DATE			

COLLECTED POEMS
1940-1978

Karl Shapiro
COLLECTED POEMS
1940-1978

Random House
New York

Some of these poems have appeared in *Evergreen Review, The New Yorker, Northwest Review, Poetry, Tri-Quarterly, Saturday Evening Post, Steppenwolf, Omnibus Chicagoland, Esquire, New Republic, California Quarterly, Poetry Now, The New York Quarterly, The Hudson Review, Audience,* and *Kayak.*

Library of Congress Cataloging in Publication Data

Shapiro, Karl Jay, 1913–
    Collected poems 1940–1978.

    Includes index.
PS3537.H2A17   1978   811'.5'2   77–90251
ISBN 0-394-42543-X

Manufactured in the United States of America

FIRST EDITION

For Teri

My thanks to David B. Robinson for help in preparation of the manuscript.

Contents

from Poems 1940–1953

from Poems of a Jew

from The Bourgeois Poet

from The Place of Love

from Selected Poems (1968)

from White-Haired Lover

New and Uncollected Poems

from Adult Bookstore

from
Person,
Place
and
Thing

The Dome of Sunday

With focus sharp as Flemish-painted face
In film of varnish brightly fixed
And through a polished hand-lens deeply seen,
Sunday at noon through hyaline thin air
Sees down the street,
And in the camera of my eye depicts
Row-houses and row-lives:
Glass after glass, door after door the same,
Face after face the same, the same,
The brutal visibility the same;

As if one life emerging from one house
Would pause, a single image caught between
Two facing mirrors where vision multiplies
Beyond perspective,
A silent clatter in the high-speed eye
Spinning out photo-circulars of sight.

I see slip to the curb the long machines
Out of whose warm and windowed rooms pirouette
Shellacked with silk and light
The hard legs of our women.
Our women are one woman, dressed in black.
The carmine printed mouth
And cheeks as soft as muslin-glass belong
Outright to one dark dressy man,
Merely a swagger at her curvy side.
This is their visit to themselves:
All day from porch to porch they weave
A nonsense pattern through the even glare,
Stealing in surfaces
Cold vulgar glances at themselves.

And high up in the heated room all day
I wait behind the plate glass pane for one,
Hot as a voyeur for a glimpse of one,
The vision to blot out this woman's sheen;
All day my sight records expensively
Row-houses and row-lives.

But nothing happens; no diagonal
With melting shadow falls across the curb:
Neither the blinded negress lurching through fatigue,
Nor exiles bleeding from their pores,
Nor that bright bomb slipped lightly from its rack
To splinter every silvered glass and crystal prism,
Witch-bowl and perfume bottle
And billion candle-power dressing-bulb,
No direct hit to smash the shatter-proof
And lodge at last the quivering needle
Clean in the eye of one who stands transfixed
In fascination of her brightness.

Washington Cathedral

From summer and the wheel-shaped city
That sweats like a swamp and wrangles on
Its melting streets, white mammoth Forums,
And political hotels with awnings, caryatids;
Past barricaded embassies with trees
That shed trash and parch his eyes,
To here, the acres of superior quiet,
Shadow and damp, the tourist comes,
And, cooled by stones and darkness, stares.

Tall as a lover's night, the nave
Broods over him, irradiates,
And stars of color out of painted glass
Shoot downward on apostles and on chairs
Huddled by hundreds under altar rails.
Yet it is only Thursday; there are no prayers,

But exclamations. The lady invokes by name
The thousand-odd small sculptures, spooks,
New angels, pitted roods; she gives
The inventory of relics to his heart
That aches with history and astonishment:
He gives a large coin to a wooden coffer.

Outside, noon blazes in his face like guns.
He goes down by the Bishop's walk, the dial,
The expensive grass, the Byzantine bench,
While stark behind him a red naked crane
Hangs over the unfinished transept,
A Cubist hen rivalling the Gothic School.

Whether he sees the joke; whether he cares;
Whether he tempts a vulgar miracle,
Some deus ex machina, this is his choice,
A shrine of whispers and tricky penumbras.
Therefore he votes again for the paid
Clergy, the English hint, the bones of Wilson
Crushed under tons of fake magnificence.
Nor from the zoo of his instincts
Come better than crude eagles: now
He cannot doubt that violent obelisk
And Lincoln whittled to a fool's colossus.
This church and city triumph in his eyes.
He is only a good alien, nominally happy.

Auto Wreck

Its quick soft silver bell beating, beating,
And down the dark one ruby flare
Pulsing out red light like an artery,
The ambulance at top speed floating down
Past beacons and illuminated clocks
Wings in a heavy curve, dips down,
And brakes speed, entering the crowd.
The doors leap open, emptying light;
Stretchers are laid out, the mangled lifted
And stowed into the little hospital.
Then the bell, breaking the hush, tolls once,
And the ambulance with its terrible cargo
Rocking, slightly rocking, moves away,
As the doors, an afterthought, are closed.

We are deranged, walking among the cops
Who sweep glass and are large and composed.
One is still making notes under the light.
One with a bucket douches ponds of blood
Into the street and gutter.
One hangs lanterns on the wrecks that cling,
Empty husks of locusts, to iron poles.

Our throats were tight as tourniquets,
Our feet were bound with splints, but now,
Like convalescents intimate and gauche,
We speak through sickly smiles and warn
With the stubborn saw of common sense,
The grim joke and the banal resolution.
The traffic moves around with care,
But we remain, touching a wound
That opens to our richest horror.
Already old, the question Who shall die?
Becomes unspoken Who is innocent?

For death in war is done by hands;
Suicide has cause and stillbirth, logic;
And cancer, simple as a flower, blooms.
But this invites the occult mind,
Cancels our physics with a sneer,
And spatters all we knew of denouement
Across the expedient and wicked stones.

Hospital

Inside or out, the key is pain. It holds
The florist to your pink medicinal rose,
The nickname to the corpse. One wipes it from
Blue German blades or drops it down the drain;
The novelist with a red tube up his nose
Gingerly pets it. Nurse can turn it off.

This is the Oxford of all sicknesses.
Kings have lain here and fabulous small Jews
And actresses whose legs were always news.
In this black room the painter lost his sight,
The crippled dancer here put down her shoes,
And the scholar's memory broke, like an old clock.

These reached to heaven and inclined their heads
While starchy angels reached them into beds:
These stooped to hell to labor out their time,
Or choked to death in seas of glaucous slime:
All tasted fire, and then, their hate annealed,
Ate sad ice-cream and wept upon a child.

What church is this, what factory of souls
Makes the bad good and fashions a new nose,
And the doctors reel with Latin and even the dead
Expect the unexpected? For O the souls
Fly back like heavy homing-birds to roost
In long-racked limbs, filling the lonely boughs.

The dead cry *life* and stagger up the hill;
But is there still the incorrigible city where
The well enjoy their poverty and the young
Worship the gutter? Is Wednesday still alive
And Tuesday wanting terribly to sin?
Hush, there are many pressing the oak doors,

Saying, "Are boys and girls important fears?
Can you predict the elections by my guts?"
But the rubber gloves are deep in a deep wound,
Stitching a single heart. These far surpass
Themselves, their wives, and the removed goiter;
Are, for the most part, human but unbandaged.

The Fly

O hideous little bat, the size of snot,
With polyhedral eye and shabby clothes,
To populate the stinking cat you walk
The promontory of the dead man's nose,
Climb with the fine leg of a Duncan-Phyfe
    The smoking mountains of my food
        And in a comic mood
    In mid-air take to bed a wife.

Riding and riding with your filth of hair
On gluey foot or wing, forever coy,
Hot from the compost and green sweet decay,
Sounding your buzzer like an urchin toy—
You dot all whiteness with diminutive stool,
    In the tight belly of the dead
        Burrow with hungry head
    And inlay maggots like a jewel.

At your approach the great horse stomps and paws
Bringing the hurricane of his heavy tail;
Shod in disease you dare to kiss my hand
Which sweeps against you like an angry flail;
Still you return, return, trusting your wing
    To draw you from the hunter's reach
        That learns to kill to teach
    Disorder to the tinier thing.

My peace is your disaster. For your death
Children like spiders cup their pretty hands
And wives resort to chemistry of war.
In fens of sticky paper and quicksands
You glue yourself to death. Where you are stuck
    You struggle hideously and beg,
        You amputate your leg
    Imbedded in the amber muck.

But I, a man, must swat you with my hate,
Slap you across the air and crush your flight,
Must mangle with my shoe and smear your blood,
Expose your little guts pasty and white,
Knock your head sidewise like a drunkard's hat,
    Pin your wings under like a crow's,
        Tear off your flimsy clothes
    And beat you as one beats a rat.

Then like Gargantua I stride among
The corpses strewn like raisins in the dust,
The broken bodies of the narrow dead
That catch the throat with fingers of disgust.
I sweep. One gyrates like a top and falls
   And stunned, stone blind, and deaf
     Buzzes its frightful F
   And dies between three cannibals.

University

To hurt the Negro and avoid the Jew
Is the curriculum. In mid-September
The entering boys, identified by hats,
Wander in a maze of mannered brick
    Where boxwood and magnolia brood
    And columns with imperious stance
    Like rows of ante-bellum girls
       Eye them, outlanders.

In whited cells, on lawns equipped for peace,
Under the arch, and lofty banister,
Equals shake hands, unequals blankly pass;
The exemplary weather whispers, "Quiet, quiet"
    And visitors on tiptoe leave
    For the raw North, the unfinished West,
    As the young, detecting an advantage,
       Practice a face.

Where, on their separate hill, the colleges,
Like manor houses of an older law,
Gaze down embankments on a land in fee,
The Deans, dry spinsters over family plate,
    Ring out the English name like coin,
    Humor the snob and lure the lout.
    Within the precincts of this world
       Poise is a club.

But on the neighboring range, misty and high,
The past is absolute: some luckless race
Dull with inbreeding and conformity
Wears out its heart, and comes barefoot and bad
    For charity or jail. The scholar
    Sanctions their obsolete disease;
    The gentleman revolts with shame
       At his ancestor.

And the true nobleman, once a democrat,
Sleeps on his private mountain. He was one
Whose thought was shapely and whose dream was broad;
This school he held his art and epitaph.
    But now it takes from him his name,
    Falls open like a dishonest look,
    And shows us, rotted and endowed,
       Its senile pleasure.

Drug Store

I do remember an apothecary,
And hereabouts 'a dwells

It baffles the foreigner like an idiom,
And he is right to adopt it as a form
Less serious than the living-room or bar;
        For it disestablishes the café,
Is a collective, and on basic country.

Not that it praises hygiene and corrupts
The ice-cream parlor and the tobacconist's
Is it a center; but that the attractive symbols
        Watch over puberty and leer
Like rubber bottles waiting for sick-use.

Youth comes to jingle nickels and crack wise;
The baseball scores are his, the magazines
Devoted to lust, the jazz, the Coca-Cola,
        The lending-library of love's latest.
He is the customer; he is heroized.

And every nook and cranny of the flesh
Is spoken to by packages with wiles.
"Buy me, buy me," they whimper and cajole;
        The hectic range of lipsticks pouts,
Revealing the wicked and the simple mouth.

With scarcely any evasion in their eye
They smoke, undress their girls, exact a stance;
But only for a moment. The clock goes round;
        Crude fellowships are made and lost;
They slump in booths like rags, not even drunk.

Haircut

O wonderful nonsense of lotions of Lucky Tiger,
Of savory soaps and oils of bottle-bright green,
The gold of liqueurs, the unguents of Newark and Niger,
Powders and balms and waters washing me clean;

In mirrors of marble and silver I see us forever
Increasing, decreasing the puzzles of luminous spaces
As I turn, am revolved and am pumped in the air on a lever,
With the backs of my heads in chorus with all of my faces.

Scissors and comb are mowing my hair into neatness,
Now pruning my ears, now smoothing my neck like a plain;
In the harvest of hair and the chaff of powdery sweetness
My snow-covered slopes grow dark with the wooly rain.

And the little boy cries, for it hurts to sever the curl,
And we too are quietly bleating to part with our coat.
Does the barber want blood in a dish? I am weak as a girl,
I desire my pendants, the fatherly chin of a goat.

I desire the pants of a bear, the nap of a monkey
Which trousers of friction have blighted down to my skin.
I am bare as a tusk, as jacketed up as a flunkey,
With the chest of a moth-eaten camel growing within.

But in death we shall flourish, you summer-dark leaves of my head,
While the flesh of the jaw ebbs away from the shores of my teeth;
You shall cover my sockets and soften the boards of my bed
And lie on the flat of my temples as proud as a wreath.

Waitress

Whoever with the compasses of his eyes
Is plotting the voyage of your steady shape
As you come laden through the room and back
And rounding your even bottom like a Cape
Crooks his first finger, whistles through his lip
Till you arrive, all motion, like a ship,

He is my friend—consider his dark pangs
And love of Niger, naked indigence,
Dance him the menu of a poem and squirm
Deep in the juke-box jungle, green and dense.
Surely he files his teeth, punctures his nose,
Carves out the god and takes off all his clothes.

For once, the token on the table's edge
Sufficing, proudly and with hair unpinned
You mounted the blueplate, stretched out and grinned
Like Christmas fish and turkey pink and skinned,
Eyes on the half-shell, loin with parsley stuck,
Thigh-bones and ribs and little toes to suck.

I speak to you, ports of the northern myth,
This dame is carved and eaten. One by one,
God knows what hour, her different parts go home,
Lastly her pants, and day or night is done;
But on the restaurant the sign of fear
Reddens and blazes—"English spoken here."

Buick

As a sloop with a sweep of immaculate wing on her delicate spine
And a keel as steel as a root that holds in the sea as she leans,
Leaning and laughing, my warm-hearted beauty, you ride, you ride,
You tack on the curves with parabola speed and a kiss of goodbye,
Like a thoroughbred sloop, my new high-spirited spirit, my kiss.

As my foot suggests that you leap in the air with your hips of a girl,
My finger that praises your wheel and announces your voices of song,
Flouncing your skirts, you blueness of joy, you flirt of politeness,
You leap, you intelligence, essence of wheelness with silvery nose,
And your platinum clocks of excitement stir like the hairs of a fern.

But how alien you are from the booming belts of your birth and the smoke
Where you turned on the stinging lathes of Detroit and Lansing at night
And shrieked at the torch in your secret parts and the amorous tests,
But now with your eyes that enter the future of roads you forget;
You are all instinct with your phosphorous glow and your streaking hair.

And now when we stop it is not as the bird from the shell that I leave
Or the leathery pilot who steps from his bird with a sneer of delight,
And not as the ignorant beast do you squat and watch me depart,
But with exquisite breathing you smile, with satisfaction of love,
And I touch you again as you tick in the silence and settle in sleep.

Israfel

la tombe de Poe éblouissante

Picture the grave in his diabolical dream
Where death would come with clues and scenery,
The bulbous forehead and the crooked mouth
Leaking a poison, the translucent hands.

Perhaps like Juliet he could come alive
To hate Longfellow and to outrage life,
But dare not from his wretched rusty stone,
Landmark for girls developing in slums.

Here he is local color, another crank;
Pawnshops and whores and sour little bars
Accept him. Neither alarming nor prophetic,
He pleases like a wop or a jack-o-lantern.

Others uptown forgive his nasty eyes
Because he was sick and had a mind to err;
But he was never dirty like Hawthorne,
But boyish with his spooks and funerals

And clammy virgins. What else were his codes
But diagrams of hideouts of the mind
Plugged up with corpses and expensive junk,
Prosopopoeia to keep himself at bay?

Think of him as a cicerone with data
False as a waxworks and that understood
Ask pitifully for pain. Or think that now
Four cities claim him as France recommended.

Mongolian Idiot

A dog that spoke, a monster born of sheep
We mercilessly kill, and kill the thought,
Yet house the parrot and let the centaur go,
These being to their nature and those not.
We laugh at apes, that never quite succeed
        At eating soup or wearing hats.

Adam had named so many but not this,
This that would name a curse when it had come,
Unfinished man, or witch, or myth, or sin,
Not ever father and never quite a son.
Ape had outstripped him, dog and darling lamb
        And all the kindergarten beasts.

Enter the bare room of his mind and count
His store of words with letters large and black;
See how he handles clumsily those blocks
With swans and sums; his colored picture books.
At thirty-five he squeals to see the ball
        Bounce in the air and roll away.

Pity and fear we give this innocent
Who maimed his mother's beautiful instinct;
But she would say, "My body had a dog;
I bore the ape and nursed the crying sheep.
He is my kindness and my splendid gift
        Come from all life and for all life."

Necropolis

Even in death they prosper; even in the death
Where lust lies senseless and pride fallow
The mouldering owners of rents and labor
Prosper and improve the high hill.

For theirs is the stone whose name is deepest cut,
Theirs the facsimile temple, theirs
The iron acanthus and the hackneyed Latin,
The boxwood rows and all the birds.

And even in death the poor are thickly herded
In intimate congestion under streets and alleys.
Look at the standard sculpture, the cheap
Synonymous slabs, the machined crosses.

Yes, even in death the cities are unplanned.
The heirs govern from the old centers;
They will not remove. And the ludicrous angels,
Remains of the poor, will never fly
But only multiply in the green grass.

My Grandmother

My grandmother moves to my mind in context of sorrow
And, as if apprehensive of near death, in black;
Whether erect in chair, her dry and corded throat harangued by grief,
Or at ragged book bent in Hebrew prayer,
Or gentle, submissive, and in tears to strangers;
Whether in sunny parlor or back of drawn blinds.

Though time and tongue made any love disparate,
On daguerreotype with classic perspective
Beauty I sigh and soften at is hers.
I pity her life of deaths, the agony of her own,
But most that history moved her through
Stranger lands and many houses,
Taking her exile for granted, confusing
The tongues and tasks of her children's children.

October 1

That season when the leaf deserts the bole
And half-dead see-saws through the October air
Falling face-downward on the walks to print
The decalcomania of its little soul—
Hardly has the milkman's sleepy horse
On wooden shoes echoed across the blocks,
When with its back jaws open like a dredge
The van comes lumbering up the curb to someone's door and knocks.

And four black genii muscular and shy
Holding their shy caps enter the first room
Where someone hurriedly surrenders up
The thickset chair, the mirror half awry,
Then to their burdens stoop without a sound.
One with his bare hands rends apart the bed,
One stuffs the china-barrel with stale print,
Two bear the sofa toward the door with dark funereal tread.

The corner lamp, the safety eye of night,
Enveloped in the sun blinks and goes blind
And soon the early risers pick their way
Through kitchenware and pillows bolt upright.
The bureau on the sidewalk with bare back
And wrinkling veneer is most disgraced,
The sketch of Paris suffers in the wind,
Only the bike, its nose against the wall, does not show haste.

Two hours—the movers mop their necks and look,
Filing through dust and echoes back and forth.
The halls are hollow and all the floors are cleared
Bare to the last board, to the most secret nook;
But on the street a small chaos survives
That slowly now the leviathan ingests,
And schoolboys and stenographers stare at
The truck, the house, the husband in his hat who stands and rests.

He turns with miserable expectant face
And for the last time enters. On the wall
A picture-stain spreads from the nail-hole down.
Each object live and dead has left its trace.
He leaves his key; but as he quickly goes
This question comes behind: Did someone die?
Is someone rich or poor, better or worse?
What shall uproot a house and bring this care into his eye?

19

Epitaph for John and Richard

There goes the clock; there goes the sun;
Greenwich is right with Arlington;
The signal's minutes are signifying
That somebody old has finished dying,
That somebody young has just begun.

What do you think you earned today
Except the waste, except the pay,
Except the power to be spending?
And now your year is striking, ending,
What do you think you have put away?

Only a promise, only a life
Squandered in secret with a wife
In bedtime feigning and unfeigning;
The blood has long since ceased complaining;
The clock has satisfied the strife.

They will not cast your honored head
Or say from lecterns what you said,
But only keep you with them all
Committed in the City Hall;
Once born, once married, and once dead.

Emporium

He must have read Aladdin who rubbed his head
And brought this out of space; some genie came
With bolts of lawn and rugs of heavy red,
Shoes for white boxes, gems for velvet trays;
    For who could authorize in his right name
Such pricelessness of time and recklessness of days?

Not Faust, who longed for Hell, would sell his light
For moving stairs and mirrors set in miles
Where wives might wander with their sex in sight;
Rage and rat's-logic this man must have known
    Who built these buttresses on rotted piles,
Initialed every brick, and carved his lips in stone.

As if the ancient principle obtained
And solvent time would underwrite his debt,
Or the strong face of flesh were not profaned
For mannikins with hair of cloth-of-gold;
    As if no tongue had ever questioned yet
Who buys and who is bought, who sells and who is sold.

But those politely dressed in normal drab
Shall think of him remotely, think with shame
How of their skill, their goodness and their gab
He trained his joys to be obsequious Jews;
    At last not even wives shall goad his name
To feats of wealth, humility, and sickness-news;

So that, with rounded ruins honored, like Stonehenge,
Time shall have time, and he his impotent revenge.

Elegy Written on a Frontporch

The sun burns on its sultry wick;
Stratus and cumulus unite.
I who am neither well nor sick
Sit in a wicker chair and write.

A hot wind presses at my lips.
I peel. Am totally undressed.
Pinkish, as through a part-eclipse,
Heat licks upon my naked breast.

Angles in quick succession rise.
Eyesight is stereopticon
As roof and roof geometrize
Perspective deviously drawn.

I face a heaven half-destroyed,
A skyscape alabaster, dead.
One living shadow on the void,
A Flying Fortress drones ahead.

Motion and fixity take shape;
The fallow rays intensify
Distinctness. Nothing can escape
The clean hard focus of the eye.

Noise into humming noise constricts;
The traffic mumbles deeper down.
Only a trolley contradicts,
Ticks by neurotically to town.

Stretched taut upon the light I scorch,
Writhe in my sweat and smoke and sun.
The evening paper hits the porch;
My honeymoon of peace is done.

Unmasticated pulp of life . . .
Decision finds me blind and deaf.
I do not finger for the strife
Of Delano and Mutt and Jeff,

Or bend upon my nudity's
Umbilicus, the fact of facts,
As one who drowns in light and sees
The newsreel of his private acts.

I do not hug my feet with glee
And smile into my cul-de-sac
Enamoured of the dignity
Of facing forward moving back.

But set my wired sight, reclaim
The rotted friendship and the fresh;
Tune in on him who changed his name
And her who stultified the flesh.

I see who came to marriage raw
With poverty and self-abuse;
Defendants to the general law,
Their ignorance was no excuse.

Instructors, graduates I see,
Scholars who sneered into their books,
The female doctors pouring tea,
Hundreds of victims of their looks.

The money-poise of some, the pride
Of those who whored on easy checks,
Sons of The Business, dressy, snide,
Disfigured in expensive wrecks.

Believers in the songhit, thin
With pounding to the hebroid jazz;
The studious drinkers feeding in
The cloaca of the middle-class.

I see too many who romanced
Defeat, unmasculine, debased;
The striptease puritans who danced
The long lewd ritual of waste.

All these I bury out of sight
Sans benefit of epitaph.
I turn my legs into the light,
Punch out a cigarette and laugh.

For one, the best against that rout,
Deserted, obdurate to see
Their weakly literate wear out
The old Horatian fallacy;

Spoke of the beauty-to-obey,
The life-expectancy of bone.
She turned her back upon the day
But will not lie at night alone.

Death of Emma Goldman

Triumphant at the final breath,
      Their senile God, their cops,
All the authorities and friends pro tem
Passing her pillow, keeping her concerned.
But the cowardly obit was already written:
Morning would know she was a common slut.

      Russians who stood for tragedy
      Were sisters all around;
Dark conscience of the family, down she lay
To end the career of passion, brain a bruise;
And mother-wonder filled her like a tide,
Rabid and raging discipline to bear.

      In came the monarchist, a nurse,
      And covered up her eyes;
Volkstaat of hate took over: suddenly
The Ego gagged, the Conscious overpowered,
The Memory beaten to a pulp, she fell.
It remained to hide the body, or make it laugh.

      Yet not to sink her name in coin
      Like Caesar was her wish,
To come alive like Frick, conjecture maps,
Or speak with kings of low mentality,
But to be left alone, a law to scorn
Of all, and none more honored than the least.

      This way she died, though premature
      Her clarity for others;
For it was taught that, listening, the soul
Lost track and merged with trespasses and spies
Whose black renown shook money like a rat
And showed up grass a mortmain property.

The Contraband

I dreamed I held a poem and knew
The capture of a living thing.
Boys in a Grecian circle sang
And women at their harvesting.

Slowly I tried to wake and draw
The vision after, word by word,
But sleep was covetous: the song
The singers and the singing blurred.

The paper flowers of everynight
All die. Day has no counterpart,
Where memory writes its boldface wish
And swiftly punishes the heart.

Construction

The confines of a city block
Cut to a monument, exact,
At all points rectilinear,
From air a perfect square intact,

As trim as Plato thought or Eu-
Clid drew with stick. What thinker put
This idea into cubes to sell
At fifty cents a cubic foot?

O neat, O dead, what feeling thing
Could buy so bare! O dead, O neat,
What beating heart could sink to buy
The copy of the die complete!

A Robbery

By day I had dispraised their life,
Accused foremost the little cheated wives
Whose hands like trailers ludicrously hitched
To husbands, over the graph of business bump.
As often, with my friend, I laughed at them,
All but their young, whose strenuous anarchy
   Asked Why and promised war.

So of their legal dark of nights,
And bed revenge, and competent small births
That shut us out from marriage, I despaired:
Men brought home hate like evening papers, maids
Longed for their slums, the inarticulate clock
Spoke once, and faces, double-locked and still,
   Turned to the wall to sleep.

I show that fear unearthed that Boy.
Into the taut membrane of night, like knives
A woman screams, rending with rape our rest.
Bodies are ripped from beds; the snapped dream hangs:
And quick to plunge the torn portieres of sleep
We race soft-running Horror the length of halls.
   Ghouls are at every door.

Down in the hostile dark, as one,
The heavy faces point, close in, take aim,
And hands describe centripetal broad Wheels
Through which unseen a wiry robber moves.
Voices enlarge, cops clamber from the sky,
Our sudden symmetry dissolves. We laugh.
   "Nothing is caught, or lost."

Yet our emergency is lost,
Which would have, naked in the domestic night,
Brought us like actual murder to relief.
Boys have mixed blood and kissed to seal an oath.
Boys have an oath. O we were close to boys,
The salesman, the real estator, the clerk, and I,
   Their enemy, their poet.

Robber, paid agent of our hate,
I kiss my hand to you across the roofs
And jungle of back alleys where you hide.
You with your guns are like a boy I loved.
He was born dead and never had a name.
He was my little son. Night took him off.
Hard to unlearn is love.

The Snob

At what time in its little history
Did on the matrix of his brain a blow
Fall that struck like a relentless die
And left him speechless; or was it by degrees
That the algid folds of mind, caught in a pose,
                    Hardened and set like concrete,
Printing and fixing a distorted moment?

Nothing but death will smash this ugly cast
That wears its trade mark big upon its face,
A scutcheon for Greek-letter brotherhoods
Where it is weakly sworn by smiles to cow
Unequals, niggers or just Methodists.
                  His bearing is a school of thought,
But he is not funny and not unimportant.

Hollywood

Farthest from any war, unique in time
Like Athens or Baghdad, this city lies
Between dry purple mountains and the sea.
The air is clear and famous, every day
Bright as a postcard, bringing bungalows
    And sights. The broad nights advertise
For love and music and astronomy.

Heart of a continent, the hearts converge
On open boulevards where palms are nursed
With flare-pots like a grove, on villa roads
Where castles cultivated like a style
Breed fabulous metaphors in foreign stone,
    And on enormous movie lots
Where history repeats its vivid blunders.

Alice and Cinderella are most real.
Here may the tourist, quite sincere at last,
Rest from his dream of travels. All is new,
No ruins claim his awe, and permanence,
Despised like customs, fails at every turn.
    Here where the eccentric thrives,
Laughter and love are leading industries.

Luck is another. Here the bodyguard,
The parasite, the scholar are well paid,
The quack erects his alabaster office,
The moron and the genius are enshrined,
And the mystic makes a fortune quietly;
    Here all superlatives come true
And beauty is marketed like a basic food.

O can we understand it? Is it ours,
A crude whim of a beginning people,
A private orgy in a secluded spot?
Or alien like the word *harem*, or true
Like hideous Pittsburgh or depraved Atlanta?
    Is adolescence just as vile
As this its architecture and its talk?

Or are they parvenus, like boys and girls?
Or ours and happy, cleverest of all?
Yes. Yes. Though glamorous to the ignorant
This is the simplest city, a new school.
What is more nearly ours? If soul can mean
    The civilization of the brain,
This is a soul, a possible proud Florence.

Honkytonk

Taken as diagram of Mind that marks,
Led by an arrow, green perimeters
Where thoughts sip peace and garden; inward then
To suffering junctions, slums kicked by a boot,
        Arpeggios of porches:
        Decision, Anger, Pride,
Like Self-Reproach the city points to this
Its maudlin slapping heart, our origin.

Then at the outskirts of our Conscious, No
From old high-over offices beats down
On standard faces Business-mad, and girls,
Grass under sullen stone, grown pale with work;
        Yet shields with shadow this
        Disgraced like genitals
Ghetto of local sin, laughable Hell,
Night's very alley, loathed but let alone.

I say to harass projects of decorum
This is maintained by kids, police, douceurs,
And ravenous for marvels, rancid Jews.
Callow as brass, their eyes on nipples snagged,
        Snagged in the jaded hair,
        Goaded by silken legs,
They mill around, bacterial and bright,
Seeking outbreaks of pain, their bitter milk.

Who needs Revenge or Fear can buy: in bars
Murals of lust, and talk; movies for men;
A waxworks of syphilitics; shooting range,
Phrenologist and tattoo artist; all
        Quacks who apprehend
        And speak the dirty word.
But oh, ridiculously lost those four
Hymning salvation at the Burlesk door.

How elemental ions of pure joy
Convert to deadly sins, and bump like trucks
Uptown to roads instinctive to the young,
I only ask. But in and out they go
        Satanic to discover
        Imago of Unrest
Whose Ultima Thule is a general low
And obscene civics of our self-distrust.

The Birds

Wrong about birds. I cannot call
That swift, enslaved, mechanical
Come and go, come and go,
Build and feed and mate and grow
   Beautiful.
Beautiful, the poets are wrong
To love you for your turn and wheel and glide and song.

Beast of the wind, wolf of the tree,
Heart with the gunner's history,
Rise and fall, rise and fall,
Heart of the heart I cannot call
   Liberty.
Liberty, the poets are wrong
To love you for your turn and wheel and glide and song.

Elegy For Two Banjos

Haul up the flag, you mourners,
      Not half-mast but all the way;
The funeral is done and disbanded;
      The devil's had the final say.

O mistress and wife too pensive,
      Pallbearers and priestly men,
Put your black clothes in the attic,
      And get up on your feet again.

Death did his job like a scholar,
      A most unusual case,
Death did his job like a gentleman;
      He barely disturbed the face.

You packed him in a handsome carton,
      Set the lid with silver screws;
You dug a dark pit in the graveyard
      To tell the white worms the news.

Now you've nothing left to remember,
      Nothing but the words he wrote,
But they'll never let you remember,
      Only stick like a bone in your throat.

O if I'd been his wife or mistress,
      His pallbearer or his parish priest,
I'd have kept him at home forever—
      Or as long as bric-a-brac at least.

I would have burned his body
      And salvaged a sizeable bone
For a paper-weight or a door-stop
      Or a garden flagstone.

I would have heaped the fire
      And boiled his beautiful skull.
It was laden like a ship for travels
      And now is but an empty hull.

I would have dried it off in linens,
      Polished it with a chamois cloth
Till it shone like a brand-new quarter
      And felt smooth as the nose of a moth.

Or I'd have hung it out in the garden
         Where everything else is alive,
Put a queen bee in the brain case
         So the bees could build a hive.

Maybe I'd have wired the jawbone
         With a silver spring beneath,
Set it in the cradle with baby
         So baby could rattle the teeth.

O you didn't do right by William
         To shove him down that filthy hole,
Throw him a lot of tears and Latin
         And a cheap "God bless your soul."

You might as well leave off mourning,
         His photograph is getting dim,
So you'd better take a long look at it
         For it's all you'll ever see of him.

Haul up the flag, you mourners,
         Not half-mast but all the way;
The funeral is done and disbanded;
         The devil's had the final say.

Scyros

snuffle and sniff and handkerchief

The doctor punched my vein
The captain called me Cain
Upon my belly sat the sow of fear
  With coins on either eye
  The President came by
And whispered to the braid what none could hear

High over where the storm
Stood steadfast cruciform
The golden eagle sank in wounded wheels
  White Negroes laughing still
  Crept fiercely on Brazil
Turning the navies upward on their keels

Now one by one the trees
Stripped to their naked knees
To dance upon the heaps of shrunken dead
  The roof of England fell
  Great Paris tolled her bell
And China staunched her milk and wept for bread

No island singly lay
But lost its name that day
The Ainu dived across the plunging sands
  From dawn to dawn to dawn
  King George's birds came on
Strafing the tulips from his children's hands

Thus in the classic sea
Southeast from Thessaly
The dynamited mermen washed ashore
  And tritons dressed in steel
  Trolled heads with rod and reel
And dredged potatoes from the Aegean floor

Hot is the sky and green
Where Germans have been seen
The moon leaks metal on the Atlantic fields
  Pink boys in birthday shrouds
  Loop lightly through the clouds
Or coast the peaks of Finland on their shields

That prophet year by year
Lay still but could not hear
Where scholars tapped to find his new remains
Gog and Magog ate pork
In vertical New York
And war began next Wednesday on the Danes.

The Glutton

The jowls of his belly crawl and swell like the sea
When his mandibles oily with lust champ and go wide;
Eternal, the springs of his spittle leak at the lips
Suspending the tongue like a whale that rolls on the tide.

His hands are as rotten fruit. His teeth are as corn.
Deep are the wells of his eyes and like navels, blind.
Dough is the brain that supplies his passion with bread.
Dough is the loose-slung sack of his great behind.

Will his paps become woman's? He dreams of the yielding of milk,
Despising the waste of his stool that recalls him to bread;
More than passion of sex and the transverse pains of disease
He thinks of starvation, the locked-up mouth of the dead.

I am glad that his stomach will eat him away in revenge,
Digesting itself when his blubber is lain in the earth.
Let the juice of his gluttony swallow him inward like lime
And leave of his volume only the mould of his girth.

Guineapig

What do you care, dear total stranger,
For the successful failure of my safest danger,
My pig in the poke or dog in the manger,

Or who does what in the where of his chamber
Probing for his gallstones and the rods of amber
When the succubae sing and the accusers clamber?

Tooth for a Tooth, O why will you wander
After somebody's anybody's body to squander?
Do the heads grow bald as the hands grow fonder?

Thank you. Your kiss of conditional surrender
Reminds me of the case of dubious gender
Who died on the verge of gaining a defender.

Then read it and weep, dear lovelorn panther;
Change your pajamas and fill the decanter;
Down with the dreamwork and long live the banter.

Poet

Il arrive que l'esprit demande la poesie

Left leg flung out, head cocked to the right,
Tweed coat or army uniform, with book,
Beautiful eyes, who is this walking down?
Who, glancing at the pane of glass looks sharp
And thinks it is not he—as when a poet
Comes swiftly on some half-forgotten poem
And loosely holds the page, steady of mind,
       Thinking it is not his?

And when will *you* exist?—Oh, it is I,
Incredibly skinny, stooped, and neat as pie,
Ignorant as dirt, erotic as an ape,
Dreamy as puberty—with dirty hair!
Into the room like kangaroo he bounds,
Ears flopping like the most expensive hound's;
His chin receives all questions as he bows
       Mouthing a green bon-bon.

Has no more memory than rubber. Stands
Waist-deep in heavy mud of thought and broods
At his own wetness. When he would get out,
To his surprise he lifts in air a phrase
As whole and clean and silvery as a fish
Which jumps and dangles on his damned hooked grin,
But like a name-card on a man's lapel
       Calls him a conscious fool.

And child-like he remembers all his life
And cannily constructs it, fact by fact,
As boys paste postage stamps in careful books,
Denoting pence and legends and profiles,
Nothing more valuable.—And like a thief,
His eyes glassed over and congealed with guilt,
Fondles his secrets like a case of tools,
       And waits in empty doors.

By men despised for knowing what he is,
And by himself. But he exists for women.
As dolls to girls, as perfect wives to men,
So he to women. And to himself a thing,
All ages, epicene, without a trade.
To girls and wives always alive and fated;

To men and scholars always dead like Greek
        And always mistranslated.

Towards exile and towards shame he lures himself,
Tongue winding on his arm, and thinks like Eve
By biting apple will become most wise.
Sentio ergo sum: he feels his way
And words themselves stand up for him like Braille
And punch and perforate his parchment ear.
All language falls like Chinese on his soul,
        Image of song unsounded.

This is the coward's coward that in his dreams
Sees shapes of pain grow tall. Awake at night
He peers at sounds and stumbles at a breeze.
And none holds life less dear. For as a youth
Who by some accident observes his love
Naked and in some natural ugly act,
He turns with loathing and with flaming hands,
        Seared and betrayed by sight.

He is the business man, on beauty trades,
Dealer in arts and thoughts who, like the Jew,
Shall rise from slums and hated dialects
A tower of bitterness. Shall be always strange,
Hunted and then sought after. Shall be sat
Like an ambassador from another race
At tables rich with music. He shall eat flowers,
Chew honey and spit out gall. They shall all smile
        And love and pity him.

His death shall be by drowning. In that hour
When the last bubble of pure heaven's air
Hovers within his throat, safe on his bed,
A small eternal figurehead in terror,
He shall cry out and clutch his days of straw
Before the blackest wave. Lastly, his tomb
Shall list and founder in the troughs of grass
        And none shall speak his name.

Terminal

Over us stands the broad electric face
With semaphores that flick into the gaps,
Notching the time on sixtieths of space,
Springing the traveller through the folded traps
Downstairs with luggage anywhere to go
While others happily toil upward too;
Well-dressed or stricken, banished or restored,
Hundreds step down and thousands get aboard.

In neat confusion, tickets in our brain
We press the hard plush to our backs and sigh;
The brakeman thumbs his watch, the children strain
The windows to their smeary sight—Goodbye,
The great car creaks, the stone wall turns away
And lights flare past like fishes undersea;
Heads rolling heavily and all as one
With languid screams we charge into the sun.

Now through the maelstrom of the town we ride
Clicking with speed like skates on solid ice;
Streets drop and buildings silently collide,
Rails spread apart, converge and neatly splice.
Through gasping blanks of air we pound and ford
Bulking our courage forward like a road,
Climbing the world on long dead-level stairs
With catwalk stilts and trestles hung by hairs.

Out where the oaks on wide turntables grow
And constellation hamlets gyre and glow,
The straight-up bridges dive and from below
The river's sweet eccentric borders flow;
Into the culverts sliced like lands of meat,
Armies of cornstalks on their ragged feet,
And upward-outward toward the blueback hill
Where clouds of thunder graze and drink their fill.

And always at our side, swifter than we
The racing rabbits of the wire lope
And in their blood the words at liberty
Outspeed themselves; but on our rail we grope
Drinking from one white wire overhead
Hot drinks of action and hell's fiery feed.
Lightly the finger-shaped antennae feel
And lightly cheer the madness of our wheel.

We turn, we turn, thrumming the harp of sounds
And all is pleasure's move, motion of joy;
Now we imagine that we go like hounds
And now like sleds and now like many a toy
Coming alive on Christmas Day to crawl
Between the great world of the floor and wall,
But on the peak of speed we flag and fall—
Fixed on the air we do not move at all.

Arrived at space we settle in our car
And stare like souls admitted to the sky;
Nothing at length is close at hand or far;
All feats of image vanish from the eye.
Upon our brow is set the bursting star,
Upon the void the wheel and axle-bar,
The planetary fragments broken lie;
Distance is dead and light can only die.

Travelogue for Exiles

Look and remember. Look upon this sky;
Look deep and deep into the sea-clean air,
The unconfined, the terminus of prayer.
Speak now and speak into the hallowed dome.
What do you hear? What does the sky reply?
The heavens are taken: this is not your home.

Look and remember. Look upon this sea;
Look down and down into the tireless tide.
What of a life below, a life inside,
A tomb, a cradle in the curly foam?
The waves arise; sea-wind and sea agree
The waters are taken: this is not your home.

Look and remember. Look upon this land,
Far, far across the factories and the grass.
Surely, there, surely, they will let you pass.
Speak then and ask the forest and the loam.
What do you hear? What does the land command?
The earth is taken: this is not your home.

Midnight Show

The year is done, the last act of the vaudeville,
The last top hat and patent leather tappity-tap
Enclosed in darkness. Pat. Blackout. Only the organ
Groans, groans, its thousand golden throats in love;
While blue lowlight suffuses mysteries of sleep
Through racks of heads, and smoothly parts the gauzy veil
That slips, the last pretense of peace, into the wings.

With a raucous crash the music rises to its feet,
And pouring from the hidden eye like God the Light
The light white-molten cold fills out the vacant field
With shattered cities, striped ships, and maps with lines
That crawl—symbols of horror, symbols of obscenity;
A girl astride a giant cannon, holding a flag;
Removal of stone and stained-glass saints from a known cathedral;

And the Voice, the loving and faithful pointer, trots beside
Reel after reel, taking death in its well-trained stride.
The Voice, the polite, the auctioneer, places his hints
Like easy bids. The lab assistant, the Voice, dips
Their pity like litmus papers into His rancid heart.—
Dream to be surfeited, nerves clogged up with messages,
And, backed up at the ganglion, the news refused.

Dream to be out in snow where every corner Santa,
Heart of one generation's dreams, tinkles a bell.
We know him too. He is the Unemployed, but clowns
As the Giver, receiving pennies in a cast-iron pot.
Dream to be cold with Byrd at the world's bottom. Dream
To be warm in the Vatican, photographing a manuscript.
Dream to be there, a cell in Europe's poisoned blood.

Revulsion cannot rouse our heads for pride or protest.
The eye sees as the camera, a clean moronic gaze,
And to go is not impossible but merely careless.
O wife, what shall we tell the children that we saw?
O son, what shall we tell our father? And O my friend,
What shall we tell our senses when the lights go up
And noiselessly the golden curtains crash together!

Conscription Camp

Your landscape sickens with a dry disease
Even in May, Virginia, and your sweet pines
Like Frenchmen runted in a hundred wars
Are of a child's height in these battlefields.

For Wilson sowed his teeth where generals prayed
—High-sounding Lafayette and sick-eyed Lee—
The loud Elizabethan crashed your swamps
Like elephants and the subtle Indian fell.

Is it for love, you ancient-minded towns,
That on the tidy grass of your great graves
And on your roads and riverways serene
Between the corn with green flags in a row,

Wheat amorous as hair and hills like breasts
Each generation, ignorant of the last,
Mumbling in sheds, embarrassed to salute,
Comes back to choke on etiquette of hate?

You manufacture history like jute—
Labor is cheap, Virginia, for high deeds,
But in your British dream of reputation
The black man is your conscience and your cost.

Here on the plains perfect for civil war
The clapboard city like a weak mirage
Of order rises from the sand to house
These thousands and the paranoid Monroe;

The sunrise gun rasps in the throat of heaven;
The lungs of dawn are heavy and corrupt;
We hawk and spit; our flag walks through the air
Breathing hysteria thickly in each face.

Through the long school of day, absent in heart,
Distant in every thought but self we tread,
Wheeling in blocks like large expensive toys
That never understand except through fun.

To steal aside as aimlessly as curs
Is our desire; to stare at corporals
As sceptically as boys; not to believe
The misty-eyed letter and the cheap snapshot.

To cross the unnatural frontier of your name
Is our free dream, Virginia, and beyond,
White and unpatriotic in our beds,
To rise from sleep like driftwood out of surf.

But stricter than parole is this same wall
And these green clothes, a secret on the fields,
In towns betray us to the arresting touch
Of lady-wardens, good and evil wives.

And far and fabulous is the word "Outside"
Like "Europe" when the midnight liners sailed,
Leaving a wake of ermine on the tide
Where rubies drowned and eyes were softly drunk.

Still we abhor your news and every voice
Except the Personal Enemy's, and songs
That pumped by the great central heart of love
On tides of energy at evening come.

Instinctively to break your compact law
Box within box, Virginia, and throw down
The dangerous bright habits of pure form
We struggle hideously and cry for fear.

And like a very tired whore who stands
Wrapped in the sensual crimson of her art
High in the tired doorway of a street
And beckons half-concealed the passerby,

The sun, Virginia, on your Western stairs
Pauses and smiles away between the trees,
Motioning the soldier overhill to town
To his determined hungry burst of joy.

The Twins

Likeness has made them animal and shy.
See how they turn their full gaze left and right,
Seeking the other, yet not moving close;
Nothing in their relationship is gross,
But soft, conspicuous, like giraffes. And why
Do they not speak except by sudden sight?

Sisters kiss freely and unsubtle friends
Wrestle like lovers; brothers loudly laugh:
These in a dreamier bondage dare not touch.
Each is the other's soul and hears too much
The heartbeat of the other; each apprehends
The sad duality and the imperfect half.

The one lay sick, the other wandered free,
But like a child to a small plot confined
Walked a short way and dumbly reappeared.
Is it not all-in-all of what they feared,
The single death, the obvious destiny
That maims the miracle their will designed?

For they go emptily from face to face,
Keeping the instinctive partnership of birth
A ponderous marriage and a sacred name;
Theirs is the pride of shouldering each the same
The old indignity of Esau's race
And Dromio's denouement of tragic mirth.

Giantess

When Nature once in lustful hot undress
Conceived gargantuan offspring, then would I
Have loved to live near a young giantess,
Like a voluptuous cat at a queen's feet.

To see her body flower with her desire
And freely spread out in its dreadful play,
Guess if her heart concealed some heavy fire
Whose humid smokes would swim upon her eye;

To feel at leisure her stupendous shapes,
Crawl on the cliffs of her enormous knees,
And, when the unhealthy summer suns fatigued,

Have her stretch out across the plains and so
Sleep in the shadows of her breasts at ease
Like a small hamlet at a mountain's base.

(Baudelaire translation)

Blindmen

Consider them, my soul, the frightful blind!
Like mannikins, ridiculous, unbowed,
Singular, terrible, like somnambulists,
Darting their eyeballs overcast with cloud.

Their eyes from which the holy light has fled
As if far off they see, always look up;
Upon the stones of streets never look down
Inclining wearily their weighted heads. . . .

This way traverse the ever-enduring Dark,
Brother of Silence.—O Metropolis,
When all about you laugh and shout your song

With pleasure seized before this very wrong,
I cry, "I also drag myself behind!
What do they seek in Heaven, the truly blind?"

(Baudelaire translation)

Nostalgia

My soul stands at the window of my room,
    And I ten thousand miles away;
My days are filled with Ocean's sound of doom,
    Salt and cloud and the bitter spray.
Let the wind blow, for many a man shall die.

My selfish youth, my books with gilded edge,
    Knowledge and all gaze down the street;
The potted plants upon the window ledge
    Gaze down with selfish lives and sweet.
Let the wind blow, for many a man shall die.

My night is now her day, my day her night,
    So I lie down, and so I rise;
The sun burns close, the star is losing height,
    The clock is hunted down the skies.
Let the wind blow, for many a man shall die.

Truly a pin can make the memory bleed,
    A word explode the inward mind
And turn the skulls and flowers never freed
    Into the air, no longer blind.
Let the wind blow, for many a man shall die.

Laughter and grief join hands. Always the heart
    Clumps in the breast with heavy stride;
The face grows lined and wrinkled like a chart,
    The eyes bloodshot with tears and tide.
Let the wind blow, for many a man shall die.

A Cut Flower

I stand on slenderness all fresh and fair,
I feel root-firmness in the earth far down,
I catch in the wind and loose my scent for bees
That sack my throat for kisses and suck love.
What is the wind that brings thy body over?
Wind, I am beautiful and sick. I long
For rain that strikes and bites like cold and hurts.
Be angry, rain, for dew is kind to me
When I am cool from sleep and take my bath.

Who softens the sweet earth about my feet,
Touches my face so often and brings water?
Where does she go, taller than any sunflower
Over the grass like birds? Has she a root?
These are great animals that kneel to us,
Sent by the sun perhaps to help us grow.
I have seen death. The colors went away,
The petals grasped at nothing and curled tight.
Then the whole head fell off and left the sky.

She tended me and held me by my stalk.
Yesterday I was well, and then the gleam,
The thing sharper than frost cut me in half.
I fainted and was lifted high. I feel
Waist-deep in rain. My face is dry and drawn.
My beauty leaks into the glass like rain.
When first I opened to the sun I thought
My colors would be parched. Where are my bees?
Must I die now? Is this a part of life?

from
V-Letter
and
Other
Poems

Troop Train

It stops the town we come through. Workers raise
Their oily arms in good salute and grin.
Kids scream as at a circus. Business men
Glance hopefully and go their measured way.
And women standing at their dumbstruck door
More slowly wave and seem to warn us back,
As if a tear blinding the course of war
Might once dissolve our iron in their sweet wish.

Fruit of the world, O clustered on ourselves
We hang as from a cornucopia
In total friendliness, with faces bunched
To spray the streets with catcalls and with leers.
A bottle smashes on the moving ties
And eyes fixed on a lady smiling pink
Stretch like a rubber-band and snap and sting
The mouth that wants the drink-of-water kiss.

And on through crummy continents and days,
Deliberate, grimy, slightly drunk we crawl,
The good-bad boys of circumstance and chance,
Whose bucket-helmets bang the empty wall
Where twist the murdered bodies of our packs
Next to the guns that only seem themselves.
And distance like a strap adjusted shrinks,
Tighten across the shoulder and holds firm.

Here is a deck of cards; out of this hand
Dealer, deal me my luck, a pair of bulls,
The right draw to a flush, the one-eyed jack.
Diamonds and hearts are red but spades are black,
And spades are spades and clubs are clovers—black.
But deal me winners, souvenirs of peace.
This stands to reason and arithmetic,
Luck also travels and not all come back.

Trains lead to ships and ships to death or trains,
And trains to death or trucks, and trucks to death,
Or trucks lead to the march, the march to death,
Or that survival which is all our hope;
And death leads back to trucks and trains and ships,
But life leads to the march, O flag! at last
The place of life found after trains and death—
Nightfall of nations brilliant after war.

Hill at Parramatta

Just like a wave, the long green hill of my desire
Rides to the shore-like level here to engulf us all
Who work and joke in the hollow grave and the shallow mire
Where we must dig or else the earth will truly fall.

Long as a comber, green as grass, taut as a tent,
And there far out like specks the browsing cattle drift,
And sweet sweet with the green of life and the downhill scent,
O sweet at the heart such heavy loveliness to lift!

And you know best the void of the world, the blue and green,
And the races departing single file to the west to die—
But all your memory shines on the tiny deaths you have seen
No more nor less than the point of light in the tear of my eye:

So proud of the wave, my womanly hill, to lean on the shore
And tumble the sands and flatness of death with your silent roar.

Sydney Bridge

Though I see you, O rainbow of iron and rivetted lace
As a dancer who leaps to the music of music and light,
And poised on the pin of the moment of marvelous grace
Holds her breath in the downfall and curve of her motionless flight;

Though you walk like a queen with the stays of your womanly steel
And the pearls of your bodice are heavy with sensual pride,
And the million come under your notice and graciously kneel,
As the navies of nations come slowly to moor at your side;

Yet your pace is the pace of a man's, and your arms are outspread
In a trick of endurance to charm the demand of the bays,
And your tendons are common—the cables are coarse on your head,

You are marxist and sweaty! You grind for the labor of days;
And O sphinx of our harbor of beauty, your banner is red
And outflung at the end of the world like a silvery phrase!

Melbourne

The planted palms will keep the city warm
In any winter, and the toy Yarra flow
With boats and lovers down the grass. From walls
The flowers spring to sack the very streets
And wrought-iron tendrils curl upon the air.
The family's sex is English, and all their pain
More moderate than a long-expected death.

Yet the lipstick is poor, the girls consent
To lose their teeth and hips, and language whines
Raising the pitch to shrill humility.
At five o'clock the pubs roar on the world
And milk bars trickle pardon, as the mobs
Lunge, worse than Chicago, for the trains
Dispersing life to gardens and to tea.

Also in suburbs there is want of vice,
And even the dogs are well-behaved and nice.
Who has extracted violence like the fang,
Leaving in early minds the simile
Castration? Who watching at night the film
Suffers the technicolor King to spread
Exalted, motionless, into their dream?

For blue and diluted is this nation's eye,
Wind-worn with herding and great distances
That were not made for cities. This was a land
Laid for the park of loneliness of Earth,
And giant imagination and despair.
Who reared this sweet metropolis abides
By his own error, more profound than war.

Only my love can spare the wasted race
That worships sullenly the sordid sheep.
She shall be governor with her golden hair!
And teach the landscape laughter and destroy
With her free naked foot the matchwood quay:
Buildings themselves shall topple where she dances
And leap like frogs into the uproarious sea!

Christmas Eve: Australia

The wind blows hot. English and foreign birds
And insects different as their fish excite
The would-be calm. The usual flocks and herds
Parade in permanent quiet out of sight,
And there one crystal like a grain of light
Sticks in the crucible of day and cools.
A cloud burnt to a crisp at some great height
Sips at the dark condensing in deep pools.

I smoke and read my Bible and chew gum,
Thinking of Christ and Christmas of last year,
And what those quizzical soldiers standing near
Ask of the war and Christmases to come,
And sick of causes and the tremendous blame
Curse lightly and pronounce your serious name.

Piano

The perfect ice of the thin keys must break
And fingers crash through stillness into sound,
And through the mahogany darkness of the lake
Splinter the muteness where all notes are found.
O white face floating upwards amidst hair!
Sweet hands entangled in the golden snare,
          Escape, escape, escape,
      Or in the coils of joy be drowned.

What is the cabinet that holds such speech
And is obedient to caresses strange
As tides that stroke the long-deserted beach,
And gales that scourge the Peruvian mountain range?
O flesh of wood with flanks aglow with suns,
O quivering as at the burst of monstrous guns,
          Subside, subside, subside,
      Or into dust and atoms change.

Nor can the note-shaped heart, nor can the ear
Withstand your praise, O numbers more appalling
Than ringed and voyaging on the atmosphere
Those heavy flocks of fallen angels falling;
You strike with fists of heaven against the void
Where all but choiring music is destroyed,
          And light, and light, and light,
      Bursts into voice forever calling.

Magician

Tall in his top hat, tall and alone in the room
Of aerial music, electric light
And the click of tables, the mephistophelian man
Toys with a wand and the wonders happen—for whom
And to what end the gleam of the shellacked
Trick within trick, as plain as black and white,
And all too clever, all too matter-of-fact
Like the sudden neatness of a shutting fan?

And somewhat sinister, like a millionaire
Or a poet or a street-corner quack
With a dollar bottle of cure . . . We are drawn to his eye
Only to stop at the eye we dare not dare;
We suspect and believe; *he* looks us out of face
And seems to say that magic is the knack
Of showing the result without a trace
Of the cause, end without means, what without why.

If now the amusing audience could see
His mangey unicorn that crops
The shabby velvet of his weariness,
An inch from the abyss of villainy,
The applause would freeze, the dust settle like snow,
And long before the asbestos curtain drops
Even the children would get up to go,
Be sick in the lobby, sob with young distress;

But fortunately they cannot. We proceed
Beyond the fire-eating, doves,
Padlocks, confetti, disappearing ropes,
To personal murder, the necessary deed
Of sawing a woman in half. We want her heart.
The sable executioner in gloves
Labors, but hoc est corpus! quite apart
She stands; we applaud our disappointed hopes.

And backstage somewhere, peeling his moustache,
He muses that he is an honest man
And wonders dramatically why. Deep in his ear
At times there sounds the subterranean plash
Of Alf and Phlegeton where tides revolve
With eyes of evil. There he first began;
There is the task he can no longer solve
But only wait for till his dying year.

Red Indian

To Jim Powell

Purest of breed of all the tribes
That trekked from time and took the Trail of Tears
There to the plain beyond the bribes
Of best advantage, past the rifle's reach,
Where instinct rests and action disappears
And the skulls of cattle bleach.

High in the plateaus of their soul
The silence is reshaped like rocks by wind,
Their eyes are beads that pay their toll,
Record the race-long heritage of grief,
At altitudes where memory is thinned,
Frown like a wrinkled chief.

The painted feather still upright
They walk in concrete Tulsa dark and mute,
Their bravest blankets slashing bright
The afternoon of progress and of wives;
Their children glow like some primordial fruit
Cut from the branch by knives.

Bark-smooth as spears and arrow-straight
They watch the world like winter trees and grow;
Forests of them revive and wait,
In timeless hibernation dream and stir.
These are the lives that love the soundless snow
And wear the wind like fur.

Because their pride of nation leaps,
The august rivers where they yelled and died
Move with a blood that never sleeps.
Because their nature suffers the arrest
Of seed, their silence crowds us like a tide
And moves their mournful quest.

Nigger

And did ever a man go black with sun in a Belgian swamp,
On a feathery African plain where the sunburnt lioness lies,
And a cocoanut monkey grove where the cockatoos scratch the skies,
And the zebras striped with moonlight grasses gaze and stomp?

With a swatch of the baboon's crimson bottom cut for a lip,
And a brace of elephant ivories hung for a tusky smile,
With the muscles as level and lazy and long as the lifting Nile,
And a penis as loaded and supple and limp as the slaver's whip?

Are you beautiful still when you walk downtown in a knife-cut coat
And your yellow shoes dance at the corner curb like a brand new car,
And the buck with the arching pick looks over the new-laid tar
As you cock your eye like a cuckoo bird on a two-o'clock note?

When you got so little in steel-rim specs, when you taught that French,
When you wrote that book and you made that speech in the bottom south,
When you beat that fiddle and sang that role for Othello's mouth,
When you blew that horn for the shirt-sleeve mob and the snaky wench?

When you boxed that hun, when you raped that trash that you didn't rape,
When you caught that slug with a belly of fire and a face of gray,
When you felt that loop and you took that boot from a KKK,
And your hands hung down and your face went out in a blast of grape?

Did the Lord say yes, did the Lord say no, did you ask the Lord
When the jaw came down, when the cotton blossomed out of your bones?
Are you coming to peace, O Booker T. Lincoln Roosevelt Jones,
And is Jesus riding to raise your wage and to cut that cord?

Full Moon: New Guinea

These nights we fear the aspects of the moon,
Sleep lightly in the radiance falling clear
On palms and ferns and hills and us; for soon
The small burr of the bombers in our ear
Tickles our rest; we rise as from a nap
And take our helmets absently and meet,
Prepared for any spectacle or mishap,
At trenches fresh and narrow at our feet.

Look up, look up, and wait and breathe. These nights
We fear Orion and the Cross. The crowd
Of deadly insects caught in our long lights
Glitter and seek to burrow in a cloud
Soft-minded with high explosive. Breathe and wait,
The bombs are falling darkly for our fate.

The Gun

You were angry and manly to shatter the sleep of your throat;
The kiss of your blast is upon me, O friend of my fear,
And I savour your breath like a perfume as salt and austere
As the scent of the thunder of heaven that brims in the moat!

I grip you. We lie on the ground in the thongs of our clasp
And we stare like the hunter who starts at a tenuous cry;
We have wounded the wind with a wire and stung in the sky
A white hole that is small and unseen as the bite of the asp.

The smooth of your cheek—Do you sight from the depth of your eye
More faultless than vision, more true than the aiming of stars?
Is the heart of your hatred the target of redness of Mars
Or the roundness of heart of the one who must stumble and die?

O the valley is silent and shocked. I absolve from your name
The exaction of murder, my gun. It is I who have killed.
It is I whose enjoyment of horror is fine and fulfilled.
You are only the toy of my terror, my emblem of blame.

Come with me. We shall creep for his eyes like the sweat of my skin,
For the wind is repaired and the fallen is calling for breath.
You are only the means of the practical humor of death
Which is savage to punish the dead for the sake of my sin!

The Bed

Your clothes of snow and satin and pure blood
Are surplices of many sacraments
Full of the woven musk of birth and death,
Full of the wet wild-flower breath of marriages,
The sweat, the slow mandragora of lust.

Meadow of sleep, table of sour sickness,
Infinite road to travel, first of graves,
Your square and subtle presence rules the house,
And little wincing hurts of everyday
Clutch at your white skirt and are comforted.

What matter if you are wise or if you know?
A third of life is yours, all that we learn
We tell you, and you dream us night by night.
We take your advice, confess in sharp detail,
Add to your knowledge, yet can teach you nothing.
"Lie here," you say, and whoever we bring you, sad,
Ashamed or delighted, you take in the spirit we give.

Let me not know too much, and let your soul
Not lead me farther on than sleep and love,
For her I marry is more white than you.
Some day, as if with ancient torches stand
And fill the walls with fires around her head,
And let your gown be fresh as April grass,
And let your prothalamium be sweet.

The Second-Best Bed

In the name of the almighty God, amen,
  I, William Shakespeare, take my pen
  And do bequeath in perfect health
To Christ my soul and to my kin my wealth
      When I am dead.
      And to Anne, good dame,
      I bequeath my name,
A table, a chair, and the second-best bed.

To Judith a hundred fifty pounds I give,
  The same if three more years she live,
  And the broad-edge silver bowl. To Joan
My hose and clothes and all the suits I own
      Both blue and red.
      And to Anne, good dame,
      I bequeath my name,
A table, a chair, and the second-best bed.

Ten pounds to beggars for their drink and board,
  To Mr. Thomas Cole my sword,
  To Richard Burbage, Cundell, Nash,
Heminge and Hamlet one pound six in cash,
      And to her I wed
      Who is Anne, good dame,
      I bequeath my name,
A table, a chair, and the second-best bed.

To Joan also my Stratford house I will,
  For sisters shall not go with nil,
  And to her sons five pounds apiece
To be paid within a year of my decease.
      And as I have said
      To Anne, good dame,
      I bequeath my name,
A table, a chair, and the second-best bed.

Last, to my daughter, born Susanna Hall,
  My barns and stables, lands and all,
  Tenements, orchards, jewels, and wares,
All these forever for herself and heirs,
      Till all are dead;
      But to Anne, good dame,
      I bequeath my name,
A table, a chair, and the second-best bed.

Good wife, bad fortune is to blame
That I bequeath, when I am dead,
To you my honor and my name,
A table, a chair, and the second-best bed.

Satire: Anxiety

Alas, I would be overloved,
A sign, a Wonder unreproved,
A bronze colossus standing high
As Rhodes or famous Liberty,
Bridging with my almighty thighs
A stainless-steel metropolis
Where pigmy men in clothing creep
To Lilliputian work and sleep,
And Love with microscopic tears
Whispers to wee and perfect ears.
I would obscure the sun and throw
A shadow with my smallest toe
That down their teeming canyon files
Time could be told a hundred miles;
Lightning would flash within my hand,
An airman's beacon and sign of land,
My eyes eclipse the polar star,
Aldebaran and the flare of war;
Golden my head and cleanly hewn
Would sail above the lesser moon
And dart above the Pleiades
To peer at new astronomies
From where the earth, a bluish clod,
Seems smallest in the eye of God.

But when in lucid morning I
Survey my bulk and history,
Composite fool alive in air
With caecum and vestigial hair,
A thing of not-too-godly form
Conversant with the waiting worm,
Fixed in a span between two shades
For four or five or six decades,
Then all my pride and all my hope
As backward through a telescope
Diminish: I walk an endless street
Where topless towers for height compete,
And men of wiser blood and bone
Destroy me for the things they own—
Their taxes, vital tubes, and sons
Submissive in a world of guns.
I see my hands grow small and clear
Until they wink and disappear.

Fireworks

In midsummer darkness when primeval silences close
On the women in linen and children and husbands in blouses
We gather in laughter and move with a current that flows
Through the intimate suburbs of ice-cream and talkative houses

To a fabulous field of the night of the rainbows of ages
Where blindness is dyed with the blooms and the tints of desire,
And the wars of our boyhood rise up from the oldest of pages
With heroes erected on billboards of fuses and wire.

In the garden of pleistocene flowers we wander like Alice
Where seed sends a stalk in the heavens and pops from a pod
A blue blossom that hangs on the distance and opens its chalice
And falls in the dust of itself and goes out with a nod.

How the hairy tarantulas crawl in the soft of the ether
Where showers of lilies explode in the jungle of creepers;
How the rockets of sperm hurtle up to the moon and beneath her
Deploy for the eggs of the astral and sorrowful sleepers!

And the noble bombardment that bursts in the depth of our ears
Lifts the hair of our heads and interprets in absolute noises
The brimstone of total destruction, the doom of our years.
O the Judgment that shatters the rose of our secrets and poises!

In Niagaras of fire we leak in the luminous aura
And gasp at the portrait of Lincoln alive on the lattice.
Our history hisses and spits in the burning Gomorrah,
The volcanoes subside; we are given our liberty gratis.

Lord, I Have Seen Too Much

Lord, I have seen too much for one who sat
In quiet at his window's luminous eye
And puzzled over house and street and sky,
Safe only in the narrowest habitat;
Who studied peace as if the world were flat,
The edge of nature linear and dry,
But faltered at each brilliant entity
Drawn like a prize from some magician's hat.

Too suddenly this lightning is disclosed:
Lord, in a day the vacuum of Hell,
The mouth of blood, the ocean's ragged jaw,
More than embittered Adam ever saw
When driven from Eden to the East to dwell,
The lust of godhead hideously exposed!

Ballet Mécanique

The hand involves the wheel that weaves the hand
Without the kiss of kind; the digits flick,
The cranks obedient to no command
Raise on their iron shoulders the dead weight
For which no forges cheer. Nothing is late,
Nothing behind, excited, or too quick.
The arm involves the treadle and the wheel
Winds wakeless motion on a tireless reel.

The kiss of kind remembers wood and wool
To no cold purpose, anciently, afar:
The wheel forgets the hand that palpitates
The danceless power, and the power waits
Coiled in the tension tower for the pull
That freezes the burnt hand upon the bar.

Franklin

The star of Reason, Ben, reposed in you
Octagon spectacles, a sparking kite,
Triggers and jiggers, bobbins, reels and screws,
And aphorisms spelled in black and white.

Wiseacre, editor, and diplomat,
First of the salesmen, hero of the clerk,
The logic of invention led to bells
Joyous for George and terrible for Burke.

Poor Richard prospers and the grocery man
Has your disarming prose and pays his tax.
Sir, what is the reason for this bird
That sings and screams and coos and crows and quacks?

Two-penny buns, a whistle for the boy,
Rare Ben, the printer's devil used you well.
Lenin and Freud embroider left and right
And Curtis beats The Independence Bell.

Jefferson

If vision can dilate, my noble lord,
Farther than porticos, Italian cells,
Newtonian gardens, Haydn, and cuisine,
Tell us, most serious of all our poets,
Why is the clock so low?

I see the tender gradient of your will;
Virginia is the Florence of your soul,
Yes, ours. The architecture of your hands
Quiets ambition and revives our skill
And buys our faithlessness.

So temperate, so remote, so sure of phrase,
Your music sweeps a continent, a sphere,
Fashions a modern language for a war
And by its cadence makes responsible
Our million names to you.

When you were old the god of government
Seemed to recede a pace, and you were glad.
You watched the masons through your telescope
Finish your school of freedom. Death itself
Stood thoughtful at your bed.

And now the surfaces of mind are rubbed
Our essence starts like serum from our eyes.
How can you not assume the deities
That move behind the bloodshot look and lean
Like saints and Salem devils?

Sunday: New Guinea

The bugle sounds the measured call to prayers,
The band starts bravely with a clarion hymn,
From every side, singly, in groups, in pairs,
Each to his kind of service comes to worship Him.

Our faces washed, our hearts in the right place,
We kneel or stand or listen from our tents;
Half-naked natives with their kind of grace
Move down the road with balanced staffs like mendicants.

And over the hill the guns bang like a door
And planes repeat their mission in the heights.
The jungle outmaneuvers creeping war
And crawls within the circle of our sacred rites.

I long for our disheveled Sundays home,
Breakfast, the comics, news of latest crimes,
Talk without reference, and palindromes,
Sleep and the Philharmonic and the ponderous *Times*.

I long for lounging in the afternoons
Of clean intelligent warmth, my brother's mind,
Books and thin plates and flowers and shining spoons,
And your love's presence, snowy, beautiful, and kind.

Jew

The name is immortal but only the name, for the rest
Is a nose that can change in the weathers of time or persist
Or die out in confusion or model itself on the best.

But the name is a language itself that is whispered and hissed
Through the houses of ages, and ever a language the same,
And ever and ever a blow on our heart like a fist.

And this last of our dream in the desert, O curse of our name,
Is immortal as Abraham's voice in our fragment of prayer
Adonai, Adonai, for our bondage of murder and shame!

And the word for the murder of God will cry out on the air
Though the race is no more and the temples are closed of our will
And the peace is made fast on the earth and the earth is made fair;

Our name is impaled in the heart of the world on a hill
Where we suffer to die by the hands of ourselves, and to kill.

Shylock

*Ho, no, no, no, no, my meaning in saying he is a good
man is to have you understand me, that he is sufficient.*
—THE MERCHANT OF VENICE

Home from the court he locked the door and sat
In the evil darkness, suddenly composed.
The knife shone dimly on the table and his eyes
Like candles in an empty room
Shone hard at nothing. Yet he appeared to smile.

Then he took up his talith and his hat
And prayed mechanically and absently closed
His fingers on the knife. If he could realize
His actual defeat or personal doom
He must die or change or show that he was vile.

Nevertheless he would remain and live,
Submit to baptism, pay his fines,
Appear in the Rialto as early as tomorrow,
Not innocently but well aware
That his revenge is an accomplished fact.

And poverty itself would help to give
Humility to his old designs.
His fallen reputation would help borrow
A credit of new hate; for nothing will repair
This open breach of nature, cruel and wracked.

His daughter lies with swine, and the old rat
Tubal will be obsequious
To buy off his disgrace and bargain on his shame.
Despair can teach him nothing at all:
Gold he hates more than he hates Jesus' crown.

The logic of Balthasar will fall flat
On heaven's hearing. Incurious
As to the future, totally clear of blame,
He takes his ledgers out of the wall
And lights them with a taper and sits down.

The Synagogue

The synagogue dispirits the deep street,
Shadows the face of the pedestrian,
It is the adumbration of the Wall,
The stone survival that laments itself,
Our old entelechy of stubborn God,
Our calendar that marks a separate race.

The swift cathedral palpitates the blood,
The soul moves upward like a wing to meet
The pinnacles of saints. There flocks of thanks
In nooks of holy tracery arrive
And rested take their message in mid-air
Sphere after sphere into the papal heaven.

The altar of the Hebrews is a house,
No relic but a place, Sinai itself,
Not holy ground but factual holiness
Wherein the living god is resident.
Our scrolls are volumes of the thundered law
Sabbath by sabbath wound by hand to read.

He knows Al-Eloah to whom the Arab
Barefooted falls on sands, on table roofs,
In latticed alleys underneath the egg
On wide mosaics, when the crier shrills.
O profitable curse, most sacred rug,
Your book is blindness and your sword is rust.

And Judenhetze is the course of time;
We were rebellious, all but Abraham,
And skulked like Jonah, angry at the gourd.
Our days are captives in the minds of kings,
We stand in tens disjointed on the world
Grieving the ribbon of a coast we hated.

Some choose the ethics of belief beyond
Even particular election. Some
In bland memorial churches modify
The architecture of the state, and heaven
Disfranchised watches, caput mortuum,
The human substance eating, voting, smiling.

The Jew has no bedecked magnificat
But sits in stricken ashes after death,
Refusing grace; his grave is flowerless,
He gutters in the tallow of his name.
At Rome the multiplying tapers sing
Life endless in the history of art.

And Zion womanless refuses grace
To the first woman as to Magdalene,
But half-remembers Judith or Rahab,
The shrewd good heart of Esther honors still,
And weeps for almost sacred Ruth, but doubts
Either full harlotry or the faultless birth.

Our wine is wine, our bread is harvest bread
That feeds the body and is not the body.
Our blessing is to wine but not the blood
Nor to sangreal the sacred dish. We bless
The whiteness of the dish and bless the water
And are not anthropophagous to him.

The immanent son then came as one of us
And stood against the ark. We have no prophets,
Our scholars are afraid. There have been friars,
Great healers, poets. The stars were terrible.
At the Sadducee court he touched our panic;
We were betrayed to sacrifice this man.

We live by virtue of philosophy,
Past love, and have our devious reward.
For faith he gave us land and took the land,
Thinking us exiles of all humankind.
Our name is yet the identity of God
That storms the falling altar of the world.

The Leg

Among the iodoform, in twilight-sleep,
What have I lost? he first inquires,
Peers in the middle distance where a pain,
Ghost of a nurse, hazily moves, and day,
Her blinding presence pressing in his eyes
And now his ears. They are handling him
With rubber hands. He wants to get up.

One day beside some flowers near his nose
He will be thinking, *When will I look at it?*
And pain, still in the middle distance, will reply,
At what? and he will know it's gone,
O where! and begin to tremble and cry.
He will begin to cry as a child cries
Whose puppy is mangled under a screaming wheel.

Later, as if deliberately, his fingers
Begin to explore the stump. He learns a shape
That is comfortable and tucked in like a sock.
This has a sense of humor, this can despise
The finest surgical limb, the dignity of limping,
The nonsense of wheel-chairs. Now he smiles to the wall:
The amputation becomes an acquisition.

For the leg is wondering where he is (all is not lost)
And surely he has a duty to the leg;
He is its injury, the leg is his orphan,
He must cultivate the mind of the leg,
Pray for the part that is missing, pray for peace
In the image of man, pray, pray for its safety,
And after a little it will die quietly.

The body, what is it, Father, but a sign
To love the force that grows us, to give back
What in Thy palm is senselessness and mud?
Knead, knead the substance of our understanding
Which must be beautiful in flesh to walk,
That if Thou take me angrily in hand
And hurl me to the shark, I shall not die!

The Interlude

I

Much of transfiguration that we hear,
The ballet of the atoms, the second law
Of thermo-dynamics, Isis, and the queer

Fertilization of fish, the Catholic's awe
For the life-cycle of the Nazarene,
His wife whom sleeping Milton thought he saw;

Much of the resurrection that we've seen
And taken part in, like the Passion Play,
All of autumnal red and April green,

To those who walk in work from day to day,
To economic and responsible man,
All, all is substance. Life that lets him stay

Uses his substance kindly while she can
But drops him lifeless after his one span.

II

What lives? the proper creatures in their homes?
A weed? the white and giddy butterfly?
Bacteria? necklaces of chromosomes?

What lives? the breathing bell of the clear sky?
The crazed bull of the sea? Andean crags?
Armies that plunge into themselves to die?

People? A sacred relic wrapped in rags,
The ham-bone of a saint, the winter rose,
Do these?—And is there not a hand that drags

The bottom of the universe for those
Who still perhaps are breathing? Listen well,
There lives a quiet like a cathedral close

At the soul's center where substance cannot dwell
And life flowers like music from a bell.

III

Writing, I crushed an insect with my nail
And thought nothing at all. A bit of wing
Caught my eye then, a gossamer so frail

And exquisite, I saw in it a thing
That scorned the grossness of the thing I wrote.
It hung upon my finger like a sting.

A leg I noticed next, fine as a mote,
"And on this frail eyelash he walked," I said,
"And climbed and walked like any mountain-goat."

And in this mood I sought the little head,
But it was lost; then in my heart a fear
Cried out, "A life—why beautiful, why dead!"

It was a mite that held itself most dear,
So small I could have drowned it with a tear.

The Intellectual

What should the wars do with these jigging fools?

The man behind the book may not be man,
His own man or the book's or yet the time's,
But still be whole, deciding what he can
In praise of politics or German rimes;

But the intellectual lights a cigarette
And offers it lit to the lady, whose odd smile
Is the merest hyphen—lest he should forget
What he has been resuming all the while.

He talks to overhear, she to withdraw
To some interior feminine fireside
Where the back arches, beauty puts forth a paw
Like a black puma stretching in velvet pride,

Making him think of cats, a stray of which
Some days sets up a howling in his brain,
Pure interference such as this neat bitch
Seems to create from listening disdain.

But talk is all the value, the release,
Talk is the very fillip of an act,
The frame and subject of the masterpiece
Under whose film of age the face is cracked.

His own forehead glows like expensive wood,
But back of it the mind is disengaged,
Self-sealing clock recording bad and good
At constant temperature, intact, unaged.

But strange, his body is an open house
Inviting every passerby to stay;
The city to and fro beneath his brows
Wanders and drinks and chats from night to day.

Think of a private thought, indecent room
Where one might kiss his daughter before bed!
Life is embarrassed; shut the family tomb,
Console your neighbor for his recent dead;

Do something! die in Spain or paint a green
Gouache, go into business (Rimbaud did),

Or start another Little Magazine,
Or move in with a woman, have a kid.

Invulnerable, impossible, immune,
Do what you will, your will will not be done
But dissipate the light of afternoon
Till evening flickers like the midnight sun,

And midnight shouts and dies: I'd rather be
A milkman walking in his sleep at dawn
Bearing fat quarts of cream, and so be free,
Crossing alone and cold from lawn to lawn.

I'd rather be a barber and cut hair
Than walk with you in gilt museum halls,
You and the puma-lady, she so rare
Exhaling her silk soul upon the walls.

Go take yourselves apart, but let me be
The fault you find with everyman. I spit,
I laugh, I fight; and you, *l'homme qui rît,*
Swallow your stale saliva, and still sit.

V-Letter

I love you first because your face is fair,
        Because your eyes Jewish and blue,
Set sweetly with the touch of foreignness
Above the cheekbones, stare rather than dream.
Often your countenance recalls a boy
        Blue-eyed and small, whose silent mischief
Tortured his parents and compelled my hate
        To wish his ugly death.
Because of this reminder, my soul's trouble,
And for your face, so often beautiful,
        I love you, wish you life.

I love you first because you wait, because
        For your own sake, I cannot write
Beyond these words. I love you for these words
That sting and creep like insects and leave filth.
I love you for the poverty you cry
        And I bend down with tears of steel
That melt your hand like wax, not for this war
        The droplets shattering
Those candle-glowing fingers of my joy,
But for your name of agony, my love,
        That cakes my mouth with salt.

And all your imperfections and perfections
        And all your magnitude of grace
And all this love explained and unexplained
Is just a breath. I see you woman-size
And this looms larger and more goddess-like
        Than silver goddesses on screens.
I see you in the ugliness of light,
        Yet you are beautiful,
And in the dark of absence your full length
Is such as meets my body to the full
        Though I am starved and huge.

You turn me from these days as from a scene
        Out of an open window far
Where lies the foreign city and the war.
You are my home and in your spacious love
I dream to march as under flaring flags
        Until the door is gently shut.
Give me the tearless lesson of your pride,
        Teach me to live and die

As one deserving anonymity,
The mere devotion of a house to keep
                A woman and a man.

Give me the free and poor inheritance
                Of our own kind, not furniture
Of education, nor the prophet's pose,
The general cause of words, the hero's stance,
The ambitions incommensurable with flesh,
                But the drab makings of a room
Where sometimes in the afternoon of thought
                        The brief and blinding flash
May light the enormous chambers of your will
And show the gracious Parthenon that time
                Is ever measured by.

As groceries in a pantry gleam and smile
                Because they are important weights
Bought with the metal minutes of your pay,
So do these hours stand in solid rows,
The dowry for a use in common life.
                I love you first because your years
Lead to my matter-of-fact and simple death
                        Or to our open marriage,
And I pray nothing for my safety back,
Not even luck, because our love is whole
                Whether I live or fail.

Elegy for a Dead Soldier

I

A white sheet on the tail-gate of a truck
Becomes an altar; two small candlesticks
Sputter at each side of the crucifix
Laid round with flowers brighter than the blood,
Red as the red of our apocalypse,
Hibiscus that a marching man will pluck
To stick into his rifle or his hat,
And great blue morning-glories pale as lips
That shall no longer taste or kiss or swear.
The wind begins a low magnificat,
The chaplain chats, the palmtrees swirl their hair,
The columns come together through the mud.

II

We too are ashes as we watch and hear
The psalm, the sorrow, and the simple praise
Of one whose promised thoughts of other days
Were such as ours, but now wholly destroyed,
The service record of his youth wiped out,
His dream dispersed by shot, must disappear.
What can we feel but wonder at a loss
That seems to point at nothing but the doubt
Which flirts our sense of luck into the ditch?
Reader of Paul who prays beside this fosse,
Shall we believe our eyes or legends rich
With glory and rebirth beyond the void?

III

For this comrade is dead, dead in the war,
A young man out of millions yet to live,
One cut away from all that war can give,
Freedom of self and peace to wander free.
Who mourns in all this sober multitude
Who did not feel the bite of it before
The bullet found its aim? This worthy flesh,
This boy laid in a coffin and reviewed—
Who has not wrapped himself in this same flag,
Heard the light fall of dirt, his wound still fresh,
Felt his eyes closed, and heard the distant brag
Of the last volley of humanity?

IV

By chance I saw him die, stretched on the ground,
A tattooed arm lifted to take the blood
Of someone else sealed in a tin. I stood
During the last delirium that stays
The intelligence a tiny moment more,
And then the strangulation, the last sound.
The end was sudden, like a foolish play,
A stupid fool slamming a foolish door,
The absurd catastrophe, half-prearranged,
And all the decisive things still left to say.
So we disbanded, angrier and unchanged,
Sick with the utter silence of dispraise.

V

We ask for no statistics of the killed,
For nothing political impinges on
This single casualty, or all those gone,
Missing or healing, sinking or dispersed,
Hundreds of thousands counted, millions lost.
More than an accident and less than willed
Is every fall, and this one like the rest.
However others calculate the cost,
To us the final aggregate is *one,*
One with a name, one transferred to the blest;
And though another stoops and takes the gun,
We cannot add the second to the first.

VI

I would not speak for him who could not speak
Unless my fear were true: he was not wronged,
He knew to which decision he belonged
But let it choose itself. Ripe in instinct,
Neither the victim nor the volunteer,
He followed, and the leaders could not seek
Beyond the followers. Much of this he knew;
The journey was a detour that would steer
Into the Lincoln Highway of a land
Remorselessly improved, excited, new,
And that was what he wanted. He had planned
To earn and drive. He and the world had winked.

VII

No history deceived him, for he knew
Little of times and armies not his own;
He never felt that peace was but a loan,
Had never questioned the idea of gain.
Beyond the headlines once or twice he saw
The gathering of a power by the few
But could not tell their names; he cast his vote,
Distrusting all the elected but not law.
He laughed at socialism; *on mourrait*
Pour les industriels? He shed his coat
And not for brotherhood, but for his pay.
To him the red flag marked the sewer main.

VIII

Above all else he loathed the homily,
The slogan and the ad. He paid his bill,
But not for Congressmen at Bunker Hill.
Ideals were few and those there were not made
For conversation. He belonged to church
But never spoke of God. The Christmas tree,
The Easter egg, baptism, he observed,
Never denied the preacher on his perch,
And would not sign Resolved That or Whereas.
Softness he had and hours and nights reserved
For thinking, dressing, dancing to the jazz.
His laugh was real, his manners were homemade.

IX

Of all men poverty pursued him least;
He was ashamed of all the down and out,
Spurned the panhandler like an uneasy doubt,
And saw the unemployed as a vague mass
Incapable of hunger or revolt.
He hated other races, south or east,
And shoved them to the margin of his mind.
He could recall the justice of the Colt,
Take interest in a gang-war like a game.
His ancestry was somewhere far behind
And left him only his peculiar name.
Doors opened, and he recognized no class.

X

His children would have known a heritage,
Just or unjust, the richest in the world,
The quantum of all art and science curled
In the horn of plenty, bursting from the horn,
A people bathed in honey, Paris come,
Vienna transferred with the highest wage,
A World's Fair spread to Phoenix, Jacksonville,
Earth's capital, the new Byzantium,
Kingdom of man—who knows? Hollow or firm,
No man can ever prophesy until
Out of our death some undiscovered germ,
Whole toleration or pure peace is born.

XI

The time to mourn is short that best becomes
The military dead. We lift and fold the flag,
Lay bare the coffin with its written tag,
And march away. Behind, four others wait
To lift the box, the heaviest of loads.
The anesthetic afternoon benumbs,
Sickens our senses, forces back our talk.
We know that others on tomorrow's roads
Will fall, ourselves perhaps, the man beside,
Over the world the threatened, all who walk:
And could we mark the grave of him who died
We would write this beneath his name and date:

EPITAPH

Underneath this wooden cross there lies
A Christian killed in battle. You who read,
Remember that this stranger died in pain;
And passing here, if you can lift your eyes
Upon a peace kept by a human creed,
Know that one soldier has not died in vain.

from
Trial
of a
Poet

Homecoming

Lost in the vastness of the void Pacific
My thousand days of exile, pain,
Bid me farewell. Gone is the Southern Cross
To her own sky, fallen a continent
Under the wave, dissolved the bitterest isles
In their salt element,
And here upon the deck the mist encloses
My smile that would light up all darkness
And ask forgiveness of the things that thrust
Shame and all death on millions and on me.

We bring no raw materials from the East
But green-skinned men in blue-lit holds
And lunatics impounded between-decks;
The mighty ghoul-ship that we ride exhales
The sickly-sweet stench of humiliation,
And even the majority, untouched by steel
Or psychoneurosis, stare with eyes in rut,
Their hands a rabble to snatch the riches
Of glittering shops and girls.

Because I am angry at this kindness which
Is both habitual and contradictory
To the life of armies, now I stand alone
And hate the swarms of khaki men that crawl
Like lice upon the wrinkled hide of earth,
Infesting ships as well. Not otherwise
Could I lean outward piercing fog to find
Our sacred bridge of exile and return.
My tears are psychological, not poems
To the United States; my smile is prayer.

Gnawing the thin slops of anxiety,
Escorted by the groundswell and by gulls,
In silence and with mystery we enter
The territorial waters. Not till then
Does that convulsive terrible joy, more sudden
And brilliant than the explosion of a ship,
Shatter the tensions of the heaven and sea
To crush a hundred thousand skulls
And liberate in that high burst of love
The imprisoned souls of soldiers and of me.

The Conscientious Objector

The gates clanged and they walked you into jail
More tense than felons but relieved to find
The hostile world shut out, the flags that dripped
From every mother's windowpane, obscene
The bloodlust sweating from the public heart,
The dog authority slavering at your throat.
A sense of quiet, of pulling down the blind
Possessed you. Punishment you felt was clean.

The decks, the catwalks, and the narrow light
Composed a ship. This was a mutinous crew
Troubling the captains for plain decencies,
A Mayflower brim with pilgrims headed out
To establish new theocracies to west,
A Noah's ark coasting the topmost seas
Ten miles above the sodomites and fish.
These inmates loved the only living doves.

Like all men hunted from the world you made
A good community, voyaging the storm
To no safe Plymouth or green Ararat;
Trouble or calm, the men with Bibles prayed,
The gaunt politicals construed our hate.
The opposite of all armies, you were best
Opposing uniformity and yourselves;
Prison and personality were your fate.

You suffered not so physically but knew
Maltreatment, hunger, ennui of the mind.
Well might the soldier kissing the hot beach
Erupting in his face damn all your kind.
Yet you who saved neither yourselves nor us
Are equally with those who shed the blood
The heroes of our cause. Your conscience is
What we come back to in the armistice.

The Progress of Faust

He was born in Deutschland, as you would suspect,
And graduated in magic from Cracow
In Fifteen Five. His portraits show a brow
Heightened by science. The eye is indirect,
As of bent light upon a crooked soul,
And that he bargained with the Prince of Shame
For pleasures intellectually foul
Is known by every court that lists his name.

His frequent disappearances are put down
To visits in the regions of the damned
And to the periodic deaths he shammed,
But, unregenerate and in Doctor's gown,
He would turn up to lecture at the fair
And do a minor miracle for a fee.
Many a life he whispered up the stair
To teach the black art of anatomy.

He was as deaf to angels as an oak
When, in the fall of Fifteen Ninety-four,
He went to London and crashed through the floor
In mock damnation of the playgoing folk.
Weekending with the scientific crowd,
He met Sir Francis Bacon and helped draft
"Colours of Good and Evil" and read aloud
An obscene sermon at which no one laughed.

He toured the Continent for a hundred years
And subsidized among the peasantry
The puppet play, his tragic history;
With a white glove he boxed the devil's ears
And with a black his own. Tired of this,
He published penny poems about his sins,
In which he placed the heavy emphasis
On the white glove which, for a penny, wins.

Some time before the hemorrhage of the Kings
Of France, he turned respectable and taught;
Quite suddenly everything that he had thought
Seemed to grow scholars' beards and angels' wings.
It was the Overthrow. On Reason's throne
He sat with the fair Phrygian on his knees
And called all universities his own,
As plausible a figure as you please.

Then back to Germany as the sages' sage
To preach comparative science to the young
Who came from every land in a great throng
And knew they heard the master of the age.
When for a secret formula he paid
The Devil another fragment of his soul,
His scholars wept, and several even prayed
That Satan would restore him to them whole.

Backwardly tolerant, Faustus was expelled
From the Third Reich in Nineteen Thirty-nine.
His exit caused the breaching of the Rhine,
Except for which the frontier might have held.
Five years unknown to enemy and friend
He hid, appearing on the sixth to pose
In an American desert at war's end
Where, at his back, a dome of atoms rose.

In the Waxworks

At midday when the light rebukes the world,
Searching the seams of faces, cracks of walls
And each fault of the beautiful,
Seized by a panic of the street I fled
Into a waxworks where the elite in crime
And great in fame march past in fixed parade.
How pale they were beneath their paint, how pure
The monsters gleaming from the cubicles!

When, as in torsion, I beheld
These malformations of the evil mind
I grew serene and seemed to fall in love,
As one retiring to a moving picture
Or to a gallery of art. I saw
The basest plasm of the human soul
Here turned to sculpture, fingering,
Kissing, and corrupting life.

So back and forth among the leers of wax
I strutted for the idols of the tribe,
Aware that I was on display, not they,
And that I had come down to pray,
As one retires to a synagogue
Or to a plaster saint upon the wall.
Why were these effigies more dear to me
Than haughty mannikins in a window-shop?

I said a rosary for the Presidents
And fell upon my knees before
The Ripper and an exhibit of disease
Revolting more in its soft medium
Than in the flesh. I stroked a prince's hand,
Leaving a thumbprint in the palm. I swore
Allegiance to the suicide whose wrists
Of tallow bled with admirable red.

Why were these images more dear to me
Than faïence dolls or gods of smooth Pentelikon?
Because all statuary turns to death
And only half-art balances.
The fetish lives, idolatry is true,
The crude conception of the putrid face
Sticks to my heart. This criminal in wan
Weak cerement of translucent fat

Is my sweet saint. O heretic, O mute,
When broils efface the Metropolitan
And swinish man from some cloaca creeps
Or that deep midden, his security,
Coming to you in brutish admiration
May he look soft into your eyes;
And you, good wax, may you not then despise
Our sons and daughters, fallen apes.

D.C.

The bad breed of the natives with their hates
That border on a Georgian night,
The short vocabulary, the southern look
That writes a volume on your past, the men
Freeholders of the city-state, the women
Polite for murder—these happen to be;
The rest arrive and never quite remain.

The rest live with an easy homelessness
And common tastelessness, their souls
Weakly lit up by blazing screens and tales
Told by a newspaper. Holidays the vast
Basilicas of the railroad swallow up
Hundreds of thousands, struggling in the tide
For home, the one identity and past.

The noble riches keep themselves, the miles
Of marble breast the empty wind,
The halls of books and pictures manufacture
Their deep patinas, the fountains coldly splash
To the lone sailor, the boulevards stretch out
Farther than Arlington, where all night long
One living soldier marches for the dead.

Only the very foreign, the very proud,
The richest and the very poor
Hid in their creepy purlieus white or black
Adore this whole Augustan spectacle,
And chancelleries perceive the porch of might
Surmounted by the dome in which there lies
No Bonaparte, no Lenin, but a floor.

Yet those who govern live in quaintness, close
In the Georgian ghetto of the best;
What was the simplest of the old becomes
The exquisite palate of the new. Their names
Are admirals and paternalists, their ways
The ways of Lee who, having lost the slaves,
Died farther south, a general in the wrong.

The Convert

Deep in the shadowy bethel of the tired mind,
Where spooks and death lights ride, and Marys, too,
Materialize like senseless ectoplasm
Smiling in blue, out of the blue,
Quite gradually, on a common afternoon,
With no more inner fanfare than a sigh,
With no cross in the air, drizzle of blood,
Beauty of blinding voices from up high,
The man surrenders reason to the ghost
And enters church, via the vestry room.

The groan of positive science, hiss of friends,
Substantiate what doctors call
His rather shameful and benign disease,
But ecumenical heaven clearly sees
His love, his possibilities.
O victory of the Unintelligence,
What mystic rose developing from rock
Is more a miracle than this overthrow?
What Constitution ever promised more
Than his declared insanity?

Yet he shall be less perfect than before,
Being no longer neutral to the Book
But answerable. What formerly were poems,
Precepts, and commonplaces now are laws,
Dantean atlases, and official news.
The dust of ages settles on his mind
And in his ears he hears the click of beads
Adding, adding, adding like a prayer machine
His heartfelt sums. Upon his new-found knees
He treasures up the gold of never-ending day.

All arguments are vain—that Notre Dame
Has plumbing, Baptists shoot their fellowmen,
Hindus are pious, nuns have Cadillacs.
Apologetics anger him who is
The living proof of what he newly knows;
And proudly sorrowing for those who fail
To read his simple summa theologica,
He prays that in the burning they be spared,
And prays for mercy as the south wind blows,
And for all final sins that tip the scale.

Peace on a hundred thousand temples falls
With gently even light, revealing some
With wounded walls and missing faces, some
Spared by the bombardier, and some by God.
In mournful happiness the clerics move
To put the altars back, and the new man,
Heartbroken, walks among the broken saints,
Thinking how heavy is the hand that hates,
How light and secret is the sign of love
In the hour of many significant conversions.

Boy-Man

England's lads are miniature men
To start with, grammar in their shiny hats,
And serious: in America who knows when
Manhood begins? Presidents dance and hug
And while the kind King waves and gravely chats
America wets on England's old green rug.

The boy-man roars. Worry alone will give
This one the verisimilitude of age.
Those white teeth are his own, for he must live
Longer, grow taller than the Texas race.
Fresh are his eyes, his darkening skin the gauge
Of bloods that freely mix beneath his face.

He knows the application of the book
But not who wrote it; shuts it like a shot.
Rather than read he thinks that he will look,
Rather than look he thinks that he will talk,
Rather than talk he thinks that he will not
Bother at all; would rather ride than walk.

His means of conversation is the joke,
Humor his language underneath which lies
The undecoded dialect of the folk.
Abroad he scorns the foreigner: what's old
Is worn, what's different bad, what's odd unwise.
He gives off heat and is enraged by cold.

Charming, becoming to the suits he wears,
The boy-man, younger than his eldest son,
Inherits the state; upon his silver hairs
Time like a panama hat sits at a tilt
And smiles. To him the world has just begun
And every city waiting to be built.

Mister, remove your shoulder from the wheel
And say this prayer, "Increase my vitamins,
Make my decisions of the finest steel,
Pour motor oil upon my troubled spawn,
Forgive the Europeans for their sins,
Establish them, that values may go on."

The Voyage

The ship of my body has danced in the dance of the storm
And pierced to the center the heavy embrace of the tide;
It has plunged to the bottomless trough with the knife of its form
And leapt with the prow of its motion elate from the bride.

And now in the dawn I am salt with the taste of the wave,
Which lies with itself and suspires, her beauty asleep,
And I peer at the fishes with jaws that devour and rave
And hunt in her dream for the wrack of our hands in the deep.

But the wind is the odor of love that awakes in the sun
The stream of our voyage that lies on the belt of the seas,
And I gather and breathe in the rays of the darkness undone,
And drift in her silence of morning and sail at my ease,

Where the sponges and rubbery seaweeds and flowers of hair
Uprooted abound in the water and choke in the air.

The New Ring

The new ring oppresses the finger, embarrasses the hand, encumbers the whole arm. The free hand moves to cover the new ring, except late-at-night when the mouth reaches to kiss the soft silver, a sudden thought.

In the lodge of marriage, the secret society of love, the perfect circle binds and separates, moves and is stationary.

Till the ring becomes the flesh, leaving a white trench, and the finger is immune. For the brand is assumed. Till the flesh of the encumbered hand grows over the ring, as living wood over and around the iron spike. Till the value of the reason of the gift is coinworn, and the wound heals.

And until the wound heals, the new ring is a new nail driven through the hand upon the living wood, and the body hangs from the nail, and the nail holds.

The Southerner

He entered with the authority of politeness
And the jokes died in the air. A well-made blaze
Grew round the main log in the fireplace
Spontaneously. I watched its brightness
Spread to the altered faces of my guests.
They did not like the Southerner. I did.
A liberal felt that someone should forbid
That soft voice making its soft arrests.

As when a Negro or a prince extends
His hand to an average man, and the mind
Speeds up a minute and then drops behind,
So did the conversation of my friends.
I was amused by this respectful awe
Which those hotly deny who have no prince.
I watched the frown, the stare, and the wince
Recede into attention, the arms thaw.

I saw my southern evil memories
Raped from my mind before my eyes, my youth
Practicing caste, perfecting the untruth
Of staking honor on the wish to please.
I saw my honor's paradox:
Grandpa, the saintly Jew, keeping his beard
In difficult Virginia, yet endeared
Of blacks and farmers, although orthodox.

The nonsense of the gracious lawn,
The fall of hollow columns in the pines,
Do these deceive more than the rusted signs
Of Jesus on the road? Can they go on
In the timeless manner of all gentlefolk
There in a culture rotted and unweeded
Where the black yoni of the South is seeded
By crooked men in denims thin as silk?

They do go on, denying still the fall
Of Richmond and man, who gently live
On the street above the violence, fugitive,
Graceful, and darling, who recall
The heartbroken country once about to flower,
Full of black poison, beautiful to smell,
Who know how to conform, how to compel,
And how from the best bush to receive a flower.

Recapitulations

I

I was born downtown on a wintry day
    And under the roof where Poe expired;
Tended by nuns my mother lay
    Dark-haired and beautiful and tired.

Doctors and cousins paid their call,
    The rabbi and my father helped.
A crucifix burned on the wall
    Of the bright room where I was whelped.

At one week all my family prayed,
    Stuffed wine and cotton in my craw;
The rabbi blessed me with a blade
    According to the Mosaic Law.

The white steps blazed in Baltimore
    And cannas and white statuary.
I went home voluble and sore
    Influenced by Abraham and Mary.

II

At one the Apocalypse had spoken,
Von Moltke fell, I was housebroken.

At two how could I understand
The murder of Archduke Ferdinand?

France was involved with history,
I with my thumbs when I was three.

A sister came, we neared a war,
Paris was shelled when I was four.

I joined in our peach-kernel drive
For poison gas when I was five.

At six I cheered the big parade,
Burned sparklers and drank lemonade.

At seven I passed at school though I
Was far too young to say *Versailles*.

At eight the boom began to tire,
I tried to set our house on fire.

The Bolsheviks had drawn the line,
Lenin was stricken, I was nine.

—What evils do not retrograde
To my first odious decade?

III
Saints by whose pages I would swear,
    My Zarathustra, Edward Lear,
Ulysses, Werther, fierce Flaubert,
    Where are my books of yesteryear?

Sixteen and sixty are a pair;
    We twice live by philosophies;
My marginalia of the hair,
    Are you at one with Socrates?

Thirty subsides yet does not dare,
    Sixteen and sixty bang their fists.
How is it that I no longer care
    For Kant and the Transcendentalists?

Public libraries lead to prayer,
    EN APXH ἦν ὁ λόγος—still
Eliot and John are always there
    To tempt our admirari nil.

IV
I lived in a house of panels,
    Victorian, darkly made;
A virgin in bronze and marble
    Leered from the balustrade.

The street was a tomb of virtues,
    Autumnal for dreams and haunts;
I gazed from the polished windows
    Toward a neighborhood of aunts.

Mornings I practiced piano,
    Wrote elegies and sighed;
The evenings were conversations
    Of poetry and suicide.

Weltschmerz and mysticism,
    What tortures we undergo!
I loved with the love of Heinrich
    And the poison of Edgar Poe.

V

My first small book was nourished in the dark,
Secretly written, published, and inscribed.
Bound in wine-red, it made no brilliant mark.
Rather impossible relatives subscribed.

The best review was one I wrote myself
Under the name of a then-dearest friend.
Two hundred volumes stood upon my shelf
Saying my golden name from end to end.

I was not proud but seriously stirred;
Sorrow was song and money poetry's maid!
Sorrow I had in many a ponderous word,
But were the piper and the printer paid?

VI

The third-floor thoughts of discontented youth
Once saw the city, hardened against truth,
Get set for war. He coupled a last rime
And waited for the summons to end time.

It came. The box-like porch where he had sat,
The four bright boxes of a medium flat,
Chair he had sat in, glider where he lay
Reading the poets and prophets of his day,

He assigned abstractly to his dearest friend,
Glanced at the little street hooked at the end,
The line of poplars lately touched with spring,
Lovely as Laura, breathless, beckoning.

Mother was calm, until he left the door;
The trolley passed his sweetheart's house before

She was awake. The Armory was cold,
But naked, shivering, shocked he was enrolled.

It was the death he never quite forgot
Through the four years of death, and like as not
The true death of the best of all of us
Whose present life is largely posthumous.

VII

We waged a war within a war,
    A cause within a cause;
The glory of it was withheld
    In keeping with the laws
Whereby the public need not know
The pitfalls of the status quo.

Love was the reason for the blood:
    The black men of our land
Were seen to walk with pure white girls
    Laughing and hand in hand.
This most unreasonable state
No feeling White would tolerate.

We threw each other from the trams,
    We carried knives and pipes,
We sacrificed in self-defense
    Some of the baser types,
But though a certain number died
You would not call it fratricide.

The women with indignant tears
    Professed to love the Blacks,
And dark and wooly heads still met
    With heads of English flax.
Only the cockney could conceive
Of any marriage so naïve.

Yet scarcely fifty years before
    Their fathers rode to shoot
The undressed aborigines,
    Though not to persecute.
A fine distinction lies in that
They have no others to combat.

By order of the high command
    The black men were removed
To the interior and north;
    The crisis thus improved,
Even the women could detect
Their awful fall from intellect.

VIII

I plucked the bougainvillaea
    In Queensland in time of war;
The train stopped at the station
    And I reached it from my door.

I have never kept a flower
    And this one I never shall
I thought as I laid the blossom
    In the leaves of *Les Fleurs du Mal*.

I read my book in the desert
    In the time of death and fear,
The flower slipped from the pages
    And fell to my lap, my dear.

I sent it inside my letter,
    The purplest kiss I knew,
And thus you abused my passion
    With "A most Victorian Jew."

The Dirty Word

The dirty word hops in the cage of the mind like the Pondicherry vulture, stomping with its heavy left claw on the sweet meat of the brain and tearing it with its vicious beak, ripping and chopping the flesh. Terrified, the small boy bears the big bird of the dirty word into the house, and grunting, puffing, carries it up the stairs to his own room in the skull. Bits of black feather cling to his clothes and his hair as he locks the staring creature in the dark closet.

All day the small boy returns to the closet to examine and feed the bird, to caress and kick the bird, that now snaps and flaps its wings savagely whenever the door is opened. How the boy trembles and delights at the sight of the white excrement of the bird! How the bird leaps and rushes against the walls of the skull, trying to escape from the zoo of the vocabulary! How wildly snaps the sweet meat of the brain in its rage.

And the bird outlives the man, being freed at the man's death-funeral by a word from the rabbi.

But I one morning went upstairs and opened the door and entered the closet and found in the cage of my mind the great bird dead. Softly I wept it and softly removed it and softly buried the body of the bird in the hollyhock garden of the house I lived in twenty years before. And out of the worn black feathers of the wing have I made pens to write these elegies, for I have outlived the bird, and I have murdered it in my early manhood.

from Poems
1940-1953

Adam and Eve

I The Sickness of Adam

In the beginning, at every step, he turned
As if by instinct to the East to praise
The nature of things. Now every path was learned
He lost the lifted, almost flower-like gaze

Of a temple dancer. He began to walk
Slowly, like one accustomed to be alone.
He found himself lost in the field of talk;
Thinking became a garden of its own.

In it were new things: words he had never said,
Beasts he had never seen and knew were not
In the true garden, terrors, and tears shed
Under a tree by him, for some new thought.

And the first anger. Once he flung a staff
At softly coupling sheep and struck the ram.
It broke away. And God heard Adam laugh
And for his laughter made the creature lame.

And wanderlust. He stood upon the Wall
To search the unfinished countries lying wide
And waste, where not a living thing could crawl,
And yet he would descend, as if to hide.

His thought drew down the guardian at the gate,
To whom man said, "What danger am I in?"
And the angel, hurt in spirit, seemed to hate
The wingless thing that worried after sin,

For it said nothing but marvelously unfurled
Its wings and arched them shimmering overhead,
Which must have been the signal from the world
That the first season of our life was dead.

Adam fell down with labor in his bones,
And God approached him in the cool of day
And said, "This sickness in your skeleton
Is longing. I will remove it from your clay."

He said also, "I made you strike the sheep."
It began to rain and God sat down beside

117

The sinking man. When he was fast asleep
He wet his right hand deep in Adam's side

And drew the graceful rib out of his breast.
Far off, the latent streams began to flow
And birds flew out of Paradise to nest
On earth. Sadly the angel watched them go.

II   The Recognition of Eve

Whatever it was she had so fiercely fought
Had fled back to the sky, but still she lay
With arms outspread, awaiting its assault,
Staring up through the branches of the tree,
The fig tree. Then she drew a shuddering breath
And turned her head instinctively his way.
She had fought birth as dying men fight death.

Her sigh awakened him. He turned and saw
A body swollen, as though formed of fruits,
White as the flesh of fishes, soft and raw.
He hoped she was another of the brutes
So he crawled over and looked into her eyes,
The human wells that pool all absolutes.
It was like looking into double skies.

And when she spoke the first word (it was *thou*)
He was terror-stricken, but she raised her hand
And touched his wound where it was fading now,
For he must feel the place to understand.
Then he recalled the longing that had torn
His side, and while he watched it whitely mend,
He felt it stab him suddenly like a thorn.

He thought the woman had hurt him. Was it she
Or the same sickness seeking to return;
Or was there any difference, the pain set free
And she who seized him now as hard as iron?
Her fingers bit his body. She looked old
And involuted, like the newly-born.
He let her hurt him till she loosed her hold.

Then she forgot him and she wearily stood
And went in search of water through the grove.
Adam could see her wandering through the wood,
Studying her footsteps as her body wove
In light and out of light. She found a pool
And there he followed shyly to observe.
She was already turning beautiful.

III   The Kiss

The first kiss was with stumbling fingertips.
Their bodies grazed each other as if by chance
And touched and untouched in a kind of dance.
Second, they found out touching with their lips.

Some obscure angel, pausing on his course,
Shed such a brightness on the face of Eve
That Adam in grief was ready to believe
He had lost her love. The third kiss was by force.

Their lips formed foreign, unimagined oaths
When speaking of the Tree of Guilt. So wide
Their mouths, they drank each other from inside.
A gland of honey burst within their throats.

But something rustling hideously overhead,
They jumped up from the fourth caress and hid.

IV The Tree of Guilt

Why, on her way to the oracle of Love,
Did she not even glance up at the Tree
Of Life, that giant with the whitish cast
And glinting leaves and berries of dull gray,
As though covered with mold? But who would taste
The medicine of immortality,
And who would "be as God"? And in what way?

So she came breathless to the lowlier one
And like a priestess of the cult she knelt,
Holding her breasts in token for a sign,
And prayed the spirit of the burdened bough
That the great power of the tree be seen
And lift itself out of the Tree of Guilt
Where it had hidden in the leaves till now.

Or did she know already? Had the peacock
Rattling its quills, glancing its thousand eyes
At her, the iridescence of the dove,
Stench of the he-goat, everything that joins
Told her the mystery? It was not enough,
So from the tree the snake began to rise
And dropt its head and pointed at her loins.

She fell and hid her face and still she saw
The spirit of the tree emerge and slip
Into the open sky until it stood
Straight as a standing-stone, and spilled its seed.
And all the seed were serpents of the good.
Again the snake was seized and from its lip
It spat the venomous evil of the deed.

And it was over. But the woman lay
Stricken with what she knew, ripe in her thought
Like a fresh apple fallen from the limb
And rotten, like a fruit that lies too long.
This way she rose, ripe-rotten in her prime
And spurned the cold thing coiled against her foot
And called her husband, in a kind of song.

V   The Confession

As on the first day her first word was *thou*.
He waited while she said, "Thou art the tree."
And while she said, almost accusingly,
Looking at nothing, "Thou art the fruit I took."
She seemed smaller by inches as she spoke,
And Adam wondering touched her hair and shook,
Half understanding. He answered softly, "How?"

And for the third time, in the third way, Eve:
"The tree that rises from the middle part
Of the garden." And almost tenderly, "Thou art
The garden. *We*." Then she was overcome,
And Adam coldly, lest he should succumb
To pity, standing at the edge of doom,
Comforted her like one about to leave.

She sensed departure and she stood aside
Smiling and bitter. But he asked again,
"How did you eat? With what thing did you sin?"
And Eve with body slackened and uncouth,
"Under the tree I took the fruit of truth
From an angel. I ate it with my other mouth."
And saying so, she did not know she lied.

It was the man who suddenly released
From doubt, wept in the woman's heavy arms,
Those double serpents, subtly winding forms
That climb and drop about the manly boughs,
And dry with weeping, fiery and aroused,
Fell on her face to slake his terrible thirst
And bore her body earthward like a beast.

VI Shame

The hard blood falls back in the manly fount,
The soft door closes under Venus' mount,
The ovoid moon moves to the Garden's side
And dawn comes, but the lovers have not died.
They have not died but they have fallen apart
In sleep, like equal halves of the same heart.

How to teach shame? How to teach nakedness
To the already naked? How to express
Nudity? How to open innocent eyes
And separate the innocent from the wise?
And how to re-establish the guilty tree
In infinite gardens of humanity?

By marring the image, by the black device
Of the goat-god, by the clown of Paradise,
By fruits of cloth and by the navel's bud,
By itching tendrils and by strings of blood,
By ugliness, by the shadow of our fear,
By ridicule, by the fig-leaf patch of hair.

Whiter than tombs, whiter than whitest clay,
Exposed beneath the whitening eye of day,
They awoke and saw the covering that reveals.
They thought they were changing into animals.
Like animals they bellowed terrible cries
And clutched each other, hiding each other's eyes.

VII   Exile

The one who gave the warning with his wings,
Still doubting them, held out the sword of flame
Against the Tree of Whiteness as they came
Angrily, slowly by, like exiled kings,

And watched them at the broken-open gate
Stare in the distance long and overlong,
And then, like peasants, pitiful and strong,
Take the first step toward earth and hesitate.

For Adam raised his head and called aloud,
"My Father, who has made the garden pall,
Giving me all things and then taking all,
Who with your opposite nature has endowed

Woman, give us your hand for our descent.
Needing us greatly, even in our disgrace,
Guide us, for gladly do we leave this place
For our own land and wished-for banishment."

But woman prayed, "Guide us to Paradise."
Around them slunk the uneasy animals,
Strangely excited, uttering coughs and growls,
And bounded down into the wild abyss.

And overhead the last migrating birds,
Then empty sky. And when the two had gone
A slow half-dozen steps across the stone,
The angel came and stood among the shards

And called them, as though joyously, by name.
They turned in dark amazement and beheld
Eden ablaze with fires of red and gold,
The garden dressed for dying in cold flame,

And it was autumn, and the present world.

Israel

When I think of the liberation of Palestine,
When my eye conceives the great black English line
Spanning the world news of two thousand years,
My heart leaps forward like a hungry dog,
My heart is thrown back on its tangled chain,
My soul is hangdog in a Western chair.

When I think of the battle for Zion I hear
The drop of chains, the starting forth of feet
And I remain chained in a Western chair.
My blood beats like a bird against a wall,
I feel the weight of prisons in my skull
Falling away; my forebears stare through stone.

When I see the name of Israel high in print
The fences crumble in my flesh; I sink
Deep in a Western chair and rest my soul.
I look the stranger clear to the blue depths
Of his unclouded eye. I say my name
Aloud for the first time unconsciously.

Speak of the tillage of a million heads
No more. Speak of the evil myth no more
Of one who harried Jesus on his way
Saying, *Go faster*. Speak no more
Of the yellow badge, *secta nefaria*.
Speak the name only of the living land.

Glass Poem

The afternoon lies glazed upon the wall
And on the window shines the scene-like bay,
And on the dark reflective floor a ray
Falls, and my thoughts like ashes softly fall.

And I look up as one who looks through glass
And sees the thing his soul clearly desires,
Who stares until his vision flags and tires,
But from whose eye the image fails to pass;

Until a wish crashes the vitreous air
And comes to your real hands across this space,
Thief-like and deeply cut to touch your face,
Dearly, most bitterly to touch your hair.

And I could shatter these transparent lights,
Could thrust my arms and bring your body through,
Break from the subtle spectrum the last hue
And change my eyes to dark soft-seeing nights.

But the sun stands and the hours stare like brass
And day flows thickly into permanent time,
And toward your eyes my threatening wishes climb
Where you move through a sea of solid glass.

The Tingling Back

Sometimes deeply immured in white-washed tower
 quiet at ink and thinking book,
  alone with my own smoke,
the blood at rest, the body far below,
 swiftly there falls an angry shower
  of arrows upon my back,
like bees or electric needles run amok
 between my flesh and shirt. I know
  then I have touched the pain
of amour-propre, of something yesterday
 I said and I should not have said,
  I did and must not do.
These needles wing their insights from my brain
 and through and through my flesh they play
  to prick my skin with red
letters of shame and blue blurs of tattoo.
 I sweat and take my medicine
  for one must be sincere
and study one's sincerity like a crime:
 to be the very last to smile,
  the first one to begin
(when danger streaks the atmosphere) to fear,
 to pocket praises like a dime,
  to pet the crocodile,
to see a foreign agony as stone,
 to ravel dreams in crowded room,
  to let the hair grow tall,
to skin the eye and thrust it to the wind.
 Yet if I stood with God alone
  inside the blinding tomb
I would not feel embarrassment at all
 nor those hot needles of the mind
  which are so clean. I'd ask
not if I'd known the tissue of my will
 and scarified my body white,
  but whether, insincere,
I'd grown to the simplicity of a mask;
 and if in natural error still
  whether my fingers might
destroy the true and keep the error near.

The Minute

The office building treads the marble dark,
The mother-clock with wide and golden dial
Suffers and glows. Now is the hour of birth
Of the tremulous egg. Now is the time of correction.
O midnight, zero of eternity,
Soon on a million bureaus of the city
Will lie the new-born minute.

The new-born minute on the bureau lies,
Scratching the glass with infant kick, cutting
With diamond cry the crystal and expanse
Of timelessness. This pretty tick of death
Etches its name upon the air. I turn
Titanically in distant sleep, expelling
From my lungs the bitter gas of life.

The loathsome minute grows in length and strength,
Bending its spring to forge an iron hour
That rusts from link to link, the last one bright,
The late one dead. Between the shining works
Range the clean angels, studying that tick
Like a strange dirt, but will not pick it up
Nor move it gingerly out of harm's way.

An angel is stabbed and is carried aloft howling,
For devils have gathered on a ruby jewel
Like red mites on a berry; others arrive
To tend the points with oil and smooth the heat.
See how their vicious faces, lit with sweat,
Worship the train of wheels; see how they pull
The tape-worm Time from nothing into thing.

I with my distant heart lie wide awake
Smiling at that Swiss-perfect engine room
Driven by tiny evils. Knowing no harm
Even of gongs that loom and move in towers
And hands as high as iron masts, I sleep,
At which sad sign the angels in a flock
Rise and sweep past me, spinning threads of fear.

Love for a Hand

Two hands lie still, the hairy and the white,
And soon down ladders of reflected light
The sleepers climb in silence. Gradually
They separate on paths of long ago,
Each winding on his arm the unpleasant clew
That leads, live as a nerve, to memory.

But often when too steep her dream descends,
Perhaps to the grotto where her father bends
To pick her up, the husband wakes as though
He had forgotten something in the house.
Motionless he eyes the room that glows
With the little animals of light that prowl

This way and that. Soft are the beasts of light
But softer still her hand that drifts so white
Upon the whiteness. How like a water-plant
It floats upon the black canal of sleep,
Suspended upward from the distant deep
In pure achievement of its lovely want!

Quietly then he plucks it and it folds
And is again a hand, small as a child's.
He would revive it but it barely stirs
And so he carries it off a little way
And breaks it open gently. Now he can see
The sweetness of the fruit, his hand eats hers.

The Figurehead

Watching my paralytic friend
Caught in the giant clam of himself
Fast on the treacherous shoals of his bed,
I look away to the place he had left
Where at a decade's distance he appeared
To pause in his walk and think of a limp.
One day he arrived at the street bearing
The news that he dragged an ancient foot:
The people on their porches seemed to sway.

Though there are many wired together
In this world and the next, my friend
Strains in his clamps. He is all sprung
And locked in the rust of inner change.
The therapist who plucks him like a harp
Is a cold torture: the animal bleats
And whimpers on its far seashore
As she leans to her find with a smooth hunger.

Somewhere in a storm my pity went down:
It was a wooden figurehead
With sea-hard breasts and polished mouth.
But women wash my friend with brine
From shallow inlets of their eyes,
And women rock my friend with waves
That pulsate from the female moon.
They gather at his very edge and haul
My driftwood friend toward their fires.

Speaking of dancing, joking of sex,
I watch my paralytic friend
And seek my pity in those wastes where he
Becomes my bobbing figurehead.
Then as I take my leave I wade
Loudly into the shallows of his pain,
I splash like a vacationer,
I scare his legs and stir the time of day
With rosy clouds of sediment.

F.O. Matthiessen:
An Anniversary

To learn the meaning of his leap to death
What need to know the wounds he carried down
To his crushing sleep? For the shocked town,
Bombed by his suicide, the ejaculation of blood,
Summarized it neatly in the shibboleth
Of mutual forgiveness: Matthiessen was good.

Yet there remained a reminder on the stair
Of nothing: high on the ledge of that hotel
Where an unbalanced soldier heard the yell
Of the depraved unchristian mob to leap,
But could not, being imperfect in despair,
Jump at their will into a hell so deep,

And fell back finally in the waiting arms
Of a traffic cop, a blond girl, and a priest.
And thus the loud and thousand-handed beast
Melted away.—What mob did Matthiessen
Hear chanting in rhythm, and what uniforms
Tried to retrieve him to the world of men?

What was he saying in his heavy fall
Through space, so broken by the hand of stone?
What word was that stopped like a telephone
Torn with its nervous wire from the wall?
Does not the condemned man raise his voice to call
His phrase of justice down the empty hall?

And who betrayed him finally. Was it I?
Some poet who turned his praises into blame,
Or some historian of the parlor game
Of war? Or the easy capture of the schloss
By Slavs? The Americanization of the spy?
The death of a friend? Was there no further loss?

Left with no ground except the ground that kills,
He mourned the death of politics and died.
It was, as it were, a statesman's suicide,
For when out of the window he had flung
His life upon those uncharitable hills,
Did he not will his charity to the young?

Ego

Ego is not persona: in childhood
He rules the little senses, plays at eyes,
Betters the nose, learns warm and soft and cold,
Reacts but cannot act. Ego is old:
He fights but neither laughs nor cries,
Stares but is neither bad nor good.

Ego is not narcissus: if in youth
He lingers at the mirror, he is clear,
Is not in love and never seeks a friend,
Makes all dependent yet does not depend,
Inspects, indulges, does not fear,
Remembers all. Ego is truth.

Ego does not desire or acquire,
Is not the mouth and not the reaching hand,
Dreams never, sleeps at bedtime, rises first,
Sees that the hell of darkness is dispersed,
Is pale in winter, in summer tanned,
Functions alike in ice and fire.

Ego domesticated serves the man
But is no servant, stands aside for will,
Gives no advice, takes none. Ego can fail;
Pampered he softens, struck withdraws like snail.
Trust him to know and to keep still,
Love him as much as brother can.

A Calder

To raise an iron tree
Is a wooden irony,
But to cause it to sail
In a clean perpetual way
Is to play
Upon the spaces of the scale.
Climbing the stairs we say,
Is it work or is it play?

Alexander Calder made it
Work and play:
Leaves that will never burn
But were fired to be born,
Twigs that are stiff with life
And bend as to the magnet's breath,
Each segment back to back,
The whole a hanging burst of flak.

Still the base metals,
Touched by autumnal paint
Fall through no autumn
But, turning, feint
In a fall beyond trees,
Where forests are not wooded,
There is no killing breeze,
And iron is blooded.

French Postcard

It is so difficult not to go with it
Once it is seen. It tears the mind agape
With butcher force, with intellectual rape,
And the body hangs by a hair above the pit.

In whose brain, when the order was destroyed,
Did it take form and pose, and when the eye
Clicked, was he guillotined into the void
Where the vile emulsion hangs in strips to dry?

It rose with obvious relish to be viewed,
And lay at a sewer's mouth in the grainy dawn
Where a cop found it. It seemed a platitude
Like a bad postcard of the Parthenon.

I know its family tree, its dossier,
Its memory older than Pompeian walls.
Not that it lives but that it looks at day
Shocks. In the night, wherever it is, it calls,

And never fades, but lies flat and uncurled
Even in blast furnace at the fire's core,
Feeding fat tallow to our sunken world
Deep in the riches of our father's drawer.

The Phenomenon

How lovely it was, after the official fright,
To walk in the shadowy drifts, as if the clouds
Saturated with the obscurity of night
Had died and fallen piecemeal into shrouds.

What crepes there were, what sables heaped on stones,
What soft shakos on posts, tragically gay!
And oil-pool flooded fields that blackly shone
The more black under the liquid eye of day!

It was almost warmer to the touch than sands
And sweeter-tasting than the white, and yet
Walking, the children held their fathers' hands
Like visitors to a mine or parapet.

Then black it snowed again and while it fell
You could see the sun, an irritated rim
Wheeling through smoke; each from his shallow hell
Experienced injured vision growing dim.

But one day all was clear, and one day soon,
Sooner than those who witnessed it had died,
Nature herself forgot the phenomenon,
Her faulty snowfall brilliantly denied.

The Potomac

The thin Potomac scarcely moves
But to divide Virginia from today;
   Rider, whichever is your way
You go due south and neither South improves;
Not this, of fractured columns and queer rents
   And rags that charm the nationalist,
Not that, the axle of the continents,
Nor the thin sky that flows unprejudiced
This side and that, cleansing the poisoned breath.

   For Thomas died a Georgian death
And now the legion bones of Arlington
   Laid out in marble alphabets
Stare on the great tombs of the capitol
   Where heroes calcified and cool
   Ponder the soldier named Unknown
Whose lips are guarded with live bayonets.

   Yet he shall speak though sentries walk
And columns with their cold Corinthian stalk
   Shed gold-dust pollen on Brazil
   To turn the world to Roman chalk;
Yet he shall speak, yet he shall speak
   Whose sulphur lit the flood-lit Dome,
   Whose hands were never in the kill,
Whose will was furrows of Virginia loam.

But not like London blown apart by boys
Who learned the books of love in English schools,
His name shall strike the fluted columns down;
These shall lie buried deep as fifty Troys,
The money fade like leaves from green to brown,
And embassies dissolve to molecules.

Going to School

(Phi Beta Kappa poem, Harvard)

What shall I teach in the vivid afternoon
With the sun warming the blackboard and a slip
Of cloud catching my eye?
Only the cones and sections of the moon
Out of some flaking page of scholarship,
Only some foolish heresy
To counteract the authority of prose.
The ink runs freely and the dry chalk flows
Into the silent night of seven slates
Where I create the universe as if
It grew out of some old rabbinic glyph
Or hung upon the necessity of Yeats.

O dry imaginations, drink this dust
That grays the room and powders my coat sleeve,
For in this shaft of light
I dance upon the intellectual crust
Of our own age and hold this make-believe
Like holy-work before your sight.
This is the list of books that time has burned,
These are the lines that only poets have learned,
The frame of dreams, the symbols that dilate;
Yet when I turn from this dark exercise
I meet your bright and world-considering eyes
That build and build and never can create.

I gaze down on the garden with its green
Axial lines and scientific pond
And watch a man in white
Stiffly pursue a butterfly between
Square hedges where he takes it overhand
Into the pocket of his net.
Ah psyche, sinking in the bottled fumes,
Dragging your slow wings while the hunt resumes.
I say, "He placed an image on the pool
Of the Great Mind to float there like a leaf
And then sink downward to the dark belief
Of the Great Memory of the Hermetic School."

I say, "Linnaeus drowned the names of flowers
With the black garlands of his Latin words;
The gardens now are his,
The drug-bright blossoms of the glass are ours.

I think a million taxidermist's birds
Sing in the mind of Agassiz
Who still retained one image of the good,
Who said a fish is but a thought of God.
—This is the flat world circled by its dogs,
This is the right triangle held divine
Before bald Euclid drew his empty line
And shame fell on the ancient astrologues."

The eyes strike angles on the farther wall,
Divine geometry forms upon the page,
I feel a sense of shame.
Then as the great design begins to pall
A cock crows in a laboratory cage
And I proceed. "As for the name,
It is the potency itself of thing,
It is the power-of-rising of the wing;
Without it death and feathers, for neither reed
Of Solomon nor quill of Shakespeare's goose
Ever did more or less than to deduce
Letter from number in our ignorant creed."

And what if he who blessed these walls should walk
Invisibly in the room?—My conscience prates,
"The great biologist
Who read the universe in a piece of chalk
Said all knowledge is good, all learning waits,
And wrong hypotheses exist
To order knowledge and to set it right.
We burn, he said, that others may have light.
These are the penetralia of the school
Of the last century. Under a later sky
We call both saint and fool to prophesy
The second cycle brimming at the full."

Then the clock strikes and I erase the board,
Clearing the cosmos with a sweep of felt,
Voiding my mind as well.
Now that the blank of reason is restored
And they go talking of the crazy Celt
And ghosts that sipped his muscatel,
I must escape their laughter unaware
And sidle past the question on the stair
To gain my office. Is the image lost

138

That burned and shivered in the speculum
Or does it hover in the upper room?
Have I deceived the student or the ghost?

Here in the quiet of the book-built dark
Where masonry of volumes walls me in
I should expect to find,
Returning to me on a lower arc,
Some image bodying itself a skin,
Some object thinking forth a mind.
This search necessitates no closer look.
I close my desk and choose a modern book
And leave the building. Low, as to astound,
The sun stands with its body on the line
That separates us. Low, as to combine,
The sun touches its image to the ground.

from Poems of a Jew

The Alphabet

The letters of the Jews as strict as flames
Or little terrible flowers lean
Stubbornly upwards through the perfect ages,
Singing through solid stone the sacred names.
The letters of the Jews are black and clean
And lie in chain-line over Christian pages.
The chosen letters bristle like barbed wire
That hedge the flesh of man,
Twisting and tightening the book that warns.
These words, this burning bush, this flickering pyre
Unsacrifices the bled son of man
Yet plaits his crown of thorns.

Where go the tipsy idols of the Roman
Past synagogues of patient time,
Where go the sisters of the Gothic rose,
Where go the blue eyes of the Polish women
Past the almost natural crime,
Past the still speaking embers of ghettos,
There rise the tinder flowers of the Jews.
The letters of the Jews are dancing knives
That carve the heart of darkness seven ways.
These are the letters that all men refuse
And will refuse until the king arrives
And will refuse until the death of time
And all is rolled back in the book of days.

Messias

Alone in the darkling apartment the boy
Was reading poetry when the doorbell rang;
The sound sped to his ear and winged his joy,
The book leaped from his lap on broken wing.

Down the gilt stairwell then he peered
Where an old man of patriarchal race
Climbed in an eastern language with his beard
A black halo around his paper face.

His glasses spun with vision and his hat
Was thick with fur in the August afternoon;
His silk suit crackled heavily with light
And in his hand a rattling canister shone.

Bigger he grew and softer the root words
Of the hieratic language of his heart,
And faced the boy, who flung the entrance wide
And fled in terror from the nameless hurt.

Past every door like a dead thing he swam,
Past the entablatures of the kitchen walls,
Down the red ringing of the fire escape
Singing with sun, to the green grass he came,

Sickeningly green, leaving the man to lurch
Bewildered through the house and seat himself
In the sacrificial kitchen after his march,
To study the strange boxes on the shelf.

There mother found him mountainous and alone,
Mumbling some singsong in a monotone,
Crumbling breadcrumbs in his scholar's hand
That wanted a donation for the Holy Land.

The Confirmation

When mothers weep and fathers richly proud
Worship on Sunday morning their tall son
And girls in white like angels in a play
    Tiptoe between the potted palms
    And all the crimson windows pray,
        The preacher bound in black
Opens his hands like pages of a book
    And holds the black and crimson law
    For every boy to look.

Last night between the chapters of a dream,
The photograph still sinning in the drawer,
The boy awoke; the moon shone in the yard
    On hairy hollyhocks erect
    And buds of roses pink and hard
        And on the solid wall
A square of light like movies fell to pose
    An actress naked in the night
        As hollyhock and rose.

And to confirm his sex, breathless and white
With benediction self-bestowed he knelt
Oh tightly married to his childish grip,
    And unction smooth as holy-oil
    Fell from the vessel's level lip
        Upon the altar-cloth;
Like Easter boys the blood sang in his head
    And all night long the tallow beads
    Like tears dried in the bed.

Come from the church, you parents and you girls,
And walk with kisses and with happy jokes
Beside this man. Be doubly proud, you priest,
    Once for his passion in the rose,
    Once for his body self-released;
        And speak aloud of her
Who in the perfect consciousness of joy
    Stood naked in the electric light
    And woke the hidden boy.

The Olive Tree

Save for a lusterless honing-stone of moon
The sky stretches its flawless canopy
Blue as the blue silk of the Jewish flag
Over the valley and out to sea.
It is bluest just above the olive tree.
You cannot find in twisted Italy
So straight a one; it stands not on a crag,
Is not humpbacked with bearing in scored stone,
But perfectly erect in my front yard,
Oblivious of its fame. The fruit is hard,
Multitudinous, acid, tight on the stem;
The leaves ride boat-like in the brimming sun,
Going nowhere and scooping up the light.
It is the silver tree, the holy tree,
Tree of all attributes.
                    Now on the lawn
The olives fall by thousands, and I delight
To shed my tennis shoes and walk on them,
Pressing them coldly into the deep grass,
In love and reverence for the total loss.

The Jew at Christmas Eve

I see the thin bell-ringer standing at corners
Fine as a breath, in cloth of red,
With eyes afar and long arm of a reed
Weakly waving a religious bell,
Under the boom of caroling hours
I see the thin bell-ringer standing still,
Breasting the prosperous tide on the Christmas pave.

I see the thin bell-ringer repeating himself
From corner to corner, year to year,
Struggling to stand beneath the windy blare
Of horns that carol out of walls.
He would attract a crying waif
Or garrulous old woman down-at-heels
Or a pair of lovers on the icy pave.

Whom do you summon, Santa of the spare?
Whom do you summon, arm of a reed?
Whom do you cheer with ringing and whom chide,
And who stops at the tripod at your side
And wishes you the time of year?
A few who feed the cauldron of the unfed,
The iron cauldron on the fireless pave.

I see the thin bell-ringer as a flame
Of scarlet, trying to throw the flame
With each sweep of the bell. The tide pours on
And wets the ringer in cloth of red
And parts around the ringer of flame
With eyes afar and long arm of a reed
Who shakes the fire on the snowy pave.

The First Time

Behind shut doors, in shadowy quarantine,
There shines the lamp of iodine and rose
That stains all love with its medicinal bloom.
This boy, who is no more than seventeen,
Not knowing what to do, takes off his clothes
As one might in a doctor's anteroom.

Then in a cross-draft of fear and shame
Feels love hysterically burn away,
A candle swimming down to nothingness
Put out by its own wetted gusts of flame,
And he stands smooth as uncarved ivory
Heavily curved for some expert caress.

And finally sees the always open door
That is invisible till the time has come,
And half falls through as through a rotten wall
To where chairs twist with dragons from the floor
And the great bed drugged with its own perfume
Spreads its carnivorous flower-mouth for all.

The girl is sitting with her back to him;
She wears a black thing and she rakes her hair,
Hauling her round face upward like moonrise;
She is younger than he, her angled arms are slim
And like a country girl her feet are bare.
She watches him behind her with old eyes,

Transfixing him in space like some grotesque,
Far, far from her where he is still alone
And being here is more and more untrue.
Then she turns round, as one turns at a desk,
And looks at him, too naked and too soon,
And almost gently asks: *Are you a Jew?*

Teasing the Nuns

Up in the elevator went the nuns
    Wild as a cage of undomestic ducks,
Turning and twittering their unclipped hats,
    Gay in captivity, a flirtatious flock
Of waterfowl tipped with black
    Above the traffic and its searing suns.
Higher and higher in the wall we flew
    Hauled on by rosaries and split strands of hair,
Myself in the center sailing like Sinbad
    Yanked into heaven by a hairy Roc;
Whence we emerged into a towery cell
    Where holy cross was splayed upon the wall
In taxidermy of the eternal. They
    Bedecked in elegant bird-names dropped
Curtsies, I thought, and merrily sat
    And fixed their gaze on mine that floated out
Between them and their poised hawk.

"Sisters," I said.—And then I stopped.

The Murder of Moses

By reason of despair we set forth behind you
And followed the pillar of fire like a doubt,
To hold to belief wanted a sign,
Called the miracle of the staff and the plagues
Natural phenomena.

We questioned the expediency of the march,
Gossiped about you. What was escape
To the fear of going forward and Pharaoh's wheels?
When the chariots mired and the army flooded
Our cry of horror was one with theirs.

You always went alone, a little ahead,
Prophecy disturbed you, you were not a fanatic.
The women said you were meek, the men
Regarded you as a typical leader.
You and your black wife might have been foreigners.

We even discussed your parentage; were you really a Jew?
We remembered how Joseph had made himself a prince,
All of us shared in the recognition
Of his skill of management, sense of propriety,
Devotion to his brothers and Israel.

We hated you daily. Our children died. The water spilled.
It was as if you were trying to lose us one by one.
Our wandering seemed the wandering of your mind,
The cloud believed we were tireless,
We expressed our contempt and our boredom openly.

At last you ascended the rock; at last returned.
Your anger that day was probably His.
When we saw you come down from the mountain, your skin alight
And the stones of our law flashing,
We fled like animals and the dancers scattered.

We watched where you overturned the calf on the fire,
We hid when you broke the tablets on the rock,
We wept when we drank the mixture of gold and water.
We had hoped you were lost or had left us.
This was the day of our greatest defilement.

You were simple of heart; you were sorry for Miriam,
You reasoned with Aaron, who was your enemy.

However often you cheered us with songs and prayers
We cursed you again. The serpent bit us,
And mouth to mouth you entreated the Lord for our sake.

At the end of it all we gave you the gift of death.
Invasion and generalship were spared you.
The hand of our direction, resignedly you fell,
And while officers prepared for the river-crossing
The Old God blessed you and covered you with earth.

Though you were mortal and once committed murder
You assumed the burden of the covenant,
Spoke for the world and for our understanding.
Converse with God made you a thinker,
Taught us all early justice, made us a race.

The Crucifix
in the Filing Cabinet

Out of the filing cabinet of true steel
That saves from fire my rags of letters, bills,
Manuscripts, contracts, all the trash of praise
Which one acquires to prove and prove his days;

Out of the drawer that rolls on hidden wheels
I drew a crucifix with beaded chain,
Still new and frightened-looking and absurd.
I picked it up as one picks up a bird

And placed it on my palm. It formed a pile
Like a small mound of stones on which there stands
A tree crazy with age, and on the tree
Some ancient teacher hanging by his hands.

I found a velvet bag sewn by the Jews
For holy shawls and frontlets and soft thongs
That bind the arm at morning for great wrongs
Done in a Pharaoh's time. The crucifix

I dropped down in the darkness of this pouch,
Thought tangled with thought and chain with chain,
Till time untie the dark with greedy look,
Crumble the cross and bleed the leathery vein.

from The
Bourgeois
Poet

Solipsism

The world is my dream, says the wise child, ever so wise, not stepping on
lines. I am the world, says the wise-eyed child. I made you, mother.
I made you, sky. Take care or I'll put you back in my dream.

If I look at the sun the sun will explode, says the wicked boy. If I look
at the moon I'll drain away. Where I stay I hold them in their places.
Don't ask me what I'm doing.

The simple son was sent to science college. There he learned how everything
worked.

The one who says nothing is told everything (not that he cares). The one
who dreamed me hasn't put me back. The sun and the moon, they
rise on time. I still don't know how the engine works; I can splice a
wire. That's about it.

The dream is my world, says the sick child. I am pure as these bed sheets.
(He writes fatigue on the vast expanses.) I'm in your dream, says the
wicked boy. The simple son has been decorated for objectivity. He
who says nothing is still being told.

De Sade looks down through the bars of the Bastille. They have stepped up
the slaughter of nobles.

The Bourgeois Poet

The bourgeois poet closes the door of his study and lights his pipe. Why am I in this box, he says to himself (although it is exactly as he planned). The bourgeois poet sits down at his inoffensive desk—a door with legs, a door turned table—and almost approves the careful disarray of books, papers, magazines and such artifacts as thumbtacks. The bourgeois poet is already out of matches and gets up. It is too early in the morning for any definite emotion and the B.P. smokes. It is beautiful in the midlands: green fields and tawny fields, sorghum the color of red morocco bindings, distant new neighborhoods, cleanly and treeless, and the Veterans Hospital fronted with a shimmering Indian Summer tree. The Beep feels seasonal, placid as a melon, neat as a child's football lying under the tree, waiting for whose hands to pick it up.

The Living Rooms of My Neighbors

The living rooms of my neighbors are like beauty parlors, like night-club powder rooms, like international airport first-class lounges. The bathrooms of my neighbors are like love nests—Dufy prints, black Kleenex, furry towels, toilets so highly bred they fill and fall without a sigh (why is there no bidet in so-clean America?). The kitchens of my neighbors are like cars: what gleaming dials, what toothy enamels, engines that click and purr, idling the hours away. The basements of my neighbors are like kitchens; you could eat off the floor. Look at the furnace, spotless as a breakfront, standing alone, prize piece, the god of the household.

But I'm no different. I arrange my books with a view to their appearance. Some highbrow titles are prominently displayed. The desk in my study is carefully littered; after some thought I hang a diploma on the wall, only to take it down again. I sit at the window where I can be seen. What do my neighbors think of me—I hope they think of me. I fix the light to hit the books. I lean some rows one way, some rows another.

A man's house is his stage. Others walk on to play their bit parts. Now and again a soliloquy, a birth, an adultery.

The bars of my neighbors are various, ranging from none at all to the nearly professional, leather stools, automatic coolers, a naked painting, a spittoon for show.
The businessman, the air-force captain, the professor with tenure—it's a neighborhood with a sky.

The Wood

Wood for the fireplace, wood for the floor, what is the life span? Sometimes
before I lay the log on the fire I think: it's sculpture wood, it's walnut.
Maybe someone would find a figure in it, as children find faces in the
open fire (I never have). Then I lay it on the flames like a heretic,
where it pauses a moment, then joins in the singing. There's oak in
this cord too. My floor is oak. I watched them lay this floor, for a
vastly slower fire. The grooved pieces are fitted together; it's more like
a game than work; there are many choices. The grain falls arbitrarily,
dark streaks and light, dots and dashes, swirls and striped shields.

Dead wood can last forever (is it dead)? Dead wood glows in palaces, rosy
and dark as masterpieces. I worship wood, split my own logs in the
driveway, using a maul and iron wedges. The cracking-apart is hard
and sweet. I touch wood for my superstition, using five fingers as
an extra precaution. My gods would all be wood if I had gods, not
stone or gold or Peter's smooth-kissed toe.

In woodless Italy houses are built without a sound, no ring of hammer on
nail or wood. All is quiet, stone laid upon stone, rubble, cement, tufa,
travertine, tile. Rarely you see some show-off house of wood, exotic
among the blinding stucco, soft among the cool and stony facings, the
marbly infinitude.

Sub-Division

Orchards hang in the newspaper of sky. It's snowing names and addresses over the world, O lovely splash!

In dry percussion, hammers of prosperity practice against the too-green corn. The wheat field narrows, then disappears, leaving a memory of dry wind-waves. Who eats dry wheat but boys, wheat the hue of the backs of eighteenth-century books. Children spring from the doors where there are no trees. Roofer up there, it's been a good day.

On the oldest plains rise the newest houses, smelling of rose sawdust and nails. The clammy mortar structures itself. Everyone looks like a possible Survivor. Is he one? Is she one? Who reinvented the secret stairway, passage to the room of Poe, chapel without a god?

Christ is in voice. The mayor is pleased with the murals. The Jews next door are less noisy. Set the alarm for seven.

Rubber Plant

We pick some unsuspecting soul, usually a friend, on whom to visit a lifetime of frustration. Usually a friend, at one fell swoop. That's what friends are for.

Incapable of loyalty, I marvel at it, imitate it nicely. But the feeling comes from outside. It doesn't sprout in my own soil. I carry it from a florist of sorts, some man or woman of character, and tend it lovingly. It struggles manfully in my slant sun, flourishes in the room where I am. I scat the cat away with a loud newspaper. All my plants are exotics, bamboo, rubber, cocoa, some with names I have never found out. They do well in the hothouse of my eye; they bring admiring glances. I sketch the shadows now and then.

At the bottom of the rubber plant one great leaf is dying an interesting death. It dies with astonishing rapidity. Monday, a few dabs of bright yellow. Tuesday, a ladder of yellow on one side. Wednesday, half green, half yellow, split down the middle. Thursday a spot of deadly brown. Then the whole thing twists to a Dead Sea Scroll of deadness. A single new leaf will take a month to come.

What you say is true: I have no friends.

The Clearing

In the Clearing I am at peace. Place without memory or charm. Stores practically empty of goods, schools kindly and frightened. This Clearing is a beach without a sea.

Here there is only sporadic and symbolic violence. The clouds are all the news. Each tree is grown by hand.

By degrees, those who have ambience are alienated from the Dark Towers: the German groaning for the picture galleries; the bank director who bakes his own bread; the housewife with a flair for words who has given up bathing; the itinerant pianist with ice-blue eyes; the Siberian physicist with his smug compliments; the Oxford don with the dirtiest stories; the rabbi with the mystique of the Sabbath Queen; the bearded classicist with broken arches; the veteran bomber of three world wars. I talk to the man who brings the firewood. He gives me a wedge for a present.

The citizens of Nowhere scatter in all directions.

Upon my discharge from the Army my handwriting changed. Neat slant characters gave way to square and upright. The color of the ink no longer mattered. I met a poet who printed all his words. (I thought this dangerous.) I find I can barely read the mail that comes. Sometimes I have it read to me. I tend to misunderstand the words. My answers are brief. I still wait for the mailman, a vestigial pleasure. Mail in the Clearing is lighter.

Garrison State

Of love and death in the Garrison State I sing. From uniformed populations rises the High Art, *Oedipus King,* the Nō, the ballerina bleeding in her slippers. At the Officer's Club adultery is rationed (their children are not allowed to play with guns; this helps whet their appetite). The ladies are discussing the chemical control of behavior by radio waves: that will solve the problem of neighbors. Symposia on causes of desertion draw record-breaking crowds. The handsomer pacifists are invited to the most sought-after cocktail parties. The women try their hand at them in the rumpus room; some progress reported. Waves of asceticism sweep the automobile industry. The mere sight of a Sam Browne belt, which used to inspire contempt, brings tears to the eyes of high-school boys. All flabby citizens are automatically put under surveillance. Chess problems supersede crap in the noncoms' barracks. The sacred number is Two: two parties, two powers sworn to mutual death, two poles of everything from ethics to magnetics. It's a balanced society.

Today the order goes out: all distant places are to be abolished: beachcombers are shot like looters. Established poets are forced to wear beards and bluejeans; they are treated kindly in bohemian zoos; mysterious stipends drift their way. They can trade soap for peyote at specified libraries. Children's prizes are given for essays on the pleasures of crisis. Historians are awarded all the key posts in the foreign office. Sculptors who use old shrapnel are made the heads of schools of design. Highways move underground like veins of ore. The Anti-Sky Association (volunteer contributions only) meets naked at high noon and prays for color blindness.

"Color is a biological luxury."

Hair

One by one my troops desert. A hair at a time. One by one and there is no return. Yesterday it was dark and soft, unnoticeable as a pore. Today it sticks up at a crazy angle, bristling with what act of rebellion. Yesterday a tendril, a decoration, a vestige of biology, today barbed wire. I count them all till I've lost count. I count from the top of my head. The revolution started in that sector.

In the sole world of the self that is how it happens. One cell revolts against the general harmony. The body's bourgeois security is threatened. The government gives a perceptible shudder. One cell alone goes off, giving the finger sign of obscenity. Urchins and panhandlers cheer him on. In a moment he is making speeches. Then the police, then the militia, soon the victorious grave.

Rising crooked on my arm, darting wickedly out of my eyebrows, blanching my chest like sun, what do you want, blackmailers, professional mourners. I see you starting down my arms like lice, infiltrating to the very wrist. How far will you go? When will order be restored. Halfway measures for fops and actors, black dye, tweezers, cuticle scissors. Shall I give you away? I know your little game. I saw it in the bath the other day. This plot would tickle Rabelais. A pubic hair turned silver gray!

Carvings

Mr. Cochran flags the train. One man with a flag can stop all that steam and steel and make it roll again. He sits in a doll house by the railroad track and we go there to keep him company. All day he whittles and tells us stories. He whittles us fine sticks with designs. His favorite pattern is pitting with an awl. A stick of wood becomes a talisman with stars, indentations, smooth and magical. When we go home for our nap we show our treasures.

Two Boy Scouts climb the switch tower to pay a visit to Mr. Carter. He sits at rows of lights and black-handled levers, dangerous to touch. Everything up here is dangerous and thrilling. Mr. Carter whittles people, naked people with private parts. Sometimes there are two people stuck together in crazy positions. It's quite a museum up here. When the lift-gates clang and drop and the tràffic piles up, we all look down on the open automobiles, girls in bathing suits going to the beach. The tower trembles with the thunder of the freight train.

This figurine of steatite speaks to me. Narrow eyes, thick lips, flat nose, deep carven beard and hair, deep clover-pattern of vestment. Chalcolithic of Mohenjo-Daro.

In the junk shop I ask to buy the life-size wooden horse. It came from a saddler's of the sod-house days. But it's not for sale except to a museum. We go away, my daughter and I, with a milking stool, nice near the fireplace.

The Window Trimmer

I perform in the drug-store window, stretching into neatly folded draperies
the rubbery and lavender crepe paper. Two little children watch as I
empty a box of tacks into my mouth and tread softly between two
huge glass vessels, one filled with blue water, one filled with red. The
tack hammer is magnetized. I put it to my lips and catch a tack,
point outward, swiftly fastening the flimsy drapes this way and that.
Rosettes I make, flounces, valance at the top, then set the beautiful
cardboard actress up, life-size face selling perfume or soap. My eyes
dizzily graze her eyes.

In hardware windows comic displays of insecticides. In a thousand neighbor-
hood bars I fashion crinkly curtains of red to frame vast mirrors. Al-
ways a jocular free beer, warming off-color jokes with the woman.
Bars for workingmen. I am almost a workingman I tell myself.

I am a worker I tell myself. Ils sont dans le vrai (for I am literary). My un-
easiness with salesmen, terror of the rich. I have seven vocabularies:
they change with the locale. The city itself changes: here it is London,
here it is Paris; here it is eighteenth-century. I haunt the second-hand
bookshops or visit a one-dollar woman. It's a tossup.

Privately Printed Poems

Every day when I walk by the immense publishing company, I know they are rolling out enormous medical tomes. And I know, like a secret, they are printing my book of poems. In front of the rounded plate-glass windows I am Raskolnikov. Yet I don't affront the editor: it's purely a business transaction to him.

I want the title page just so. I show a D. H. Lawrence title page, boldface British, unmistakable. The rest in book type, untechnological. The conventional length of sixty-four pages, poetry-size. The binding maroon.

In gold I also use my middle initial but spelled out JAY. J is for Jacob. My father dropped his first name Israel. My son is named Jacob. Upper-class Jews call him Jack. My father-in-law's name was Jack, probably Jacob.

The act of a book to hold in the hand is its own reason. The little defiance of a book of poems. Bludgeoning and recompense of uncles.

Beautiful Thing

Autumn reminds me that you bit my lips, excellent nurse of the most famous
hospital, with puffy eyes and advertisable rear. North of beautiful
Baltimore, in valley taverns, reminiscent of imagined England, we
watched from the rail fence the blessing of hounds. At the place of
our date you made a pass at my just-married friend in the face of
his bride. She is dark and full, a Renoir woman with Brooklyn accent.
You are light and thin, lacking in humor or observation. How slowly
the dark one moves while you engage her husband in jokes and hugs
and public thigh-pushes, all thoroughly insincere. Till the bride's
laughter congeals in her throat and suddenly she is flying hands and
knives of fingernails slashing wickedly at your soft attractive face,
your sleepless eyes with albino lashes.

At night in the improvised bed by the living-room fire in the stone cottage
you bite and use your nails. Afterwards you want me to stay inside
you the entire night, even asleep. I laugh, I beg. Instead of whispering
darling you whisper (with such conviction) *you worm!*

Death of a Student

Down the funeral aisle ("my" student in coffin, car wreck, youngish death,
eyeglasses polished, suit pressed as if for class, except that he's dead)
come the grandparents, farmers, barely walking. Followed by yet an-
other generation—over the arm of a younging man a girl about
three asleep—drugged?—her golden pony tail flopping, asleep.

Tie tied, suit without lint, the curt sadistic sermon. Love stiffens her back.
The child evades the question, as if tossing her hair. Nihilo lies sleep-
ing.

Office Love

Office love, love of money and fight, love of calculated sex. The offices reek with thin volcanic metal. Tears fall in typewriters like drops of solder. Brimstone of brassieres, low voices, the whirr of dead-serious play. From the tropical tree and the Rothko in the Board Room to the ungrammatical broom closet fragrant with waxes, to the vast typing pool where coffee is being served by dainty waitresses maneuvering their hand trucks, music almost unnoticeable falls. The very telephones are hard and kissable, the electric water cooler sweetly sweats. Gold simmers to a boil in braceleted and sunburned cheeks. What ritual politeness nevertheless, what subtlety of clothing. And if glances meet, if shoulders graze, there's no harm done. Flowers, celebrations, pregnancy leave, how the little diamonds sparkle under the psychologically soft-colored ceilings. It's an elegant windowless world of soft pressures and efficiency joys, of civilized mishaps—mere runs in the stocking, papercuts.

Where the big boys sit the language is rougher. Phone calls to China and a private shower. No paper visible anywhere. Policy is decided by word of mouth like gangsters. There the power lies and is sexless.

High School

Waiting in front of the columnar high school (the old ones look like banks, or rather insurance companies) I glance over the top of my book. The bells go off like slow burglar alarms; innumerable sixteeners saunter out. There's no running as in the lower schools, none of that helpless gaiety of the small. Here comes a surly defiance. As in a ritual, each lights a cigaret just at the boundary where the tabu ends. Each chews. The ones in cars rev up their motors and have bad complexions like gangsters. The sixteeners are all playing gangster.

The sea of subjectivity comes at you like a tidal wave, splashing the cuffs of middle-aged monuments. War is written on their unwritten faces. They try out wet dreams and wandering mind. They're rubbing Aladdin's lamp in the locker room. They pray for moments of objectivity as drunkards pray for the one that puts you out. They've captured the telephone centers, the microphones, the magazine syndicates (they've left the movies to us). I wait behind the wheel and spy; it's enemy territory all right. My daughter comes, grows taller as she approaches. It's a moment of panic.

But once at night in the sweet and sour fall I dropped her off at the football game. The bowl of light lit up the creamy Corinthian columns. A cheer went up from the field so shrill, so young, like a thousand birds in a single cage, like a massacre of child-brides in a clearing, I felt ashamed and grave. The horror of their years stoned me to death.

The Dermatologist

The dermatologist committed suicide, a good man, a sad man, with the
hangdog mien of a proctologist.

Skin-watching, tricksy as palmistry, what medieval blips and scars, what
outcroppings of thought! Maps of remorse, tattoos from voyages
never undertaken, blueprints of literary cleverness, bad dreams of per-
sonal acid—the skin has wiles undreamed of by bacteria. Under the
living continent of skin flows molten lava; heat spots and sinkings
form, then violent eruption, appearance of crystals, the terrifying
symmetry of disease. Thus the humiliation of itch- and scratch-lust,
tearing of pleasure into pain, revenge of self and desecration of love.

So lay the mother of grown children, after the final consent to herself that
the marriage was ended. The dermatologist pronounces the name of
the rare sickness. She will lose her skin from top to toe, fingernails,
toenails. Yet she will be like new, without a scar, made perfect after
agony.

The Child Who Is Silent

The child who is silent stands against his father, lovingly looking up at him as if to say without a trace of defiance: I will speak when I have decided. He marches around the table smiling intelligently, now and then deigning to say something, perhaps "locomotive." It is somewhat frightening, a kind of rebuff to grownups. The doctors smile and shrug. If the parents are worried they don't display it. It's only like living in the last house at the edge of the subdivision. There's a bit of farm left and a highway beyond: if someone should rattle the back door in the night . . . There is a child of two minds who says nothing and who is drinking it all in. Obviously happy, very much loved, handsome and straight, laughing and playing, withholding that gift we all abuse. In that room is a tower of books with their backs to us, eloquently quiet too. Man is a torrent of language, even in death. But visitors use longer words. The little philosopher goes about his business.

This is the town where the railroads ended, the wagon trains formed in the dry gray grass. It's this frontier of speech we are always crossing. The locomotive is ridiculously dying, lumbering off to the deep clay pits to settle among the mastodon bones. The piano is thinking of Mozart. On the very top, legs crossed, at ease, sits the blue-eyed boy who holds his peace.

The Stroke

One of those idle autumn evenings on a street as harmless as an Eskimo
Pie, the young ones chatter on the porch with their aunt, a woman
of intelligence, as they say. Someone across the street has died some
days ago. Once in a while a long wail of a female voice, as though
from a quite distant bedroom. It is somber and full of dread, yet only
a phrase, a Berlioz tune. We discuss it thoroughly, how it trespasses on
the music of the street. And the aunt, taking the side of the young
perhaps, would quieten such grief, cure it more quickly, have it get up
and bathe and fill its lungs with air and look at the world, though
different now, but still the only world.

Spoken too soon. Another week and her husband dies, a man of reputation,
in excellent health. Something has drawn me to her porch again: the
family is coming from the cemetery. They carry her from the car; her
screams rip through the harmless street. Others are running from
other cars. By the end of the day half of her face is turned in paraly-
sis. For months her mouth lies in a twist—that grief that parodies a
smile.

A Poor Relation

In a single motion, a snap of the hand, you take the white bishop with
your black knight, taking-replacing. It's neat, like trigger work, the
click of the chessmen speaking in passing, like the hammers of empty
revolvers. Well, uncle who taught me the courtly game, who sat with
experts over silent boards, I never made the grade. I play as badly
now that I'm gray as I did those years before I shaved. My chess
plateau was never a high one. No matter. Still, I can beat my chil-
dren when we play, which is practically never. When we do, and I
capture a pawn or a rook with a click, taking-replacing, I think of
your house, the pipes, the dice, the trinkets, curios ("novelties" they
were called). Your business, pipes and novelties, not very lucrative
but treasure-trove of kids. Your sad blond face, so kind, politically
angry, yet easy to laugh—you were not at home in this country,
scholar manqué, drifting apart from the richer and richer relations.
Your foreign accent perhaps, your synagogue training leading to
nowhere. There was that about you of the disengaged, the saint (using
the word advisedly and well), the Jewish radiance of a Chagall. The
rich ones never played chess, the poetry of war, nor grunted sadly at
the news. In America, scholars are thrown into the street or made to
stand behind cool counters, thumping, unthumping the mighty bolts
of cloth. Good cloth at that but not for the Torah.

The Tendon

Little tendon, tiny as a hair—tinier, the surgeon said—they couldn't catch you on the operating table. Three hours we lay there, wrist neatly slit open—I can't even find the scar—while they caught you and lost you, caught you and lost you, and then, more or less sure, caught you again (but didn't).

And now one finger doesn't work so well. I can't make a fist with my left hand, and it's hard to pick up change. (I'm left-handed, of course.) It would have to be my favorite hand that I pushed through the door glass (one drink too many).

But how I slept, truth serum in my veins, happily missing the glitter and click of hemostats. And woke to your hard professional slaps in the face, in Recovery, nurse. You must have been late for your date, good-looking nurse; your make-up was perfect when I saw you at last, and you had stopped bawling my name in my ear, like a character in *Alice in Wonderland,* stopped letting me have the flat of your hand.

Arm in sling, hand in aluminum brace, I lecture and teach while the tendon sleeps. It's not worth fixing really. I'm not a pianist or, as you put it, doctor, a Swiss watchmaker. But a dancer one night says to me at a party: Are you disfigured? (Only a dancer would use a word like that.)

Editing Poetry

Next to my office where I edit poems ("Can poems be edited?") there is the Chicago Models Club. All day the girls stroll past my door where I am editing poems, behind my head a signed photograph of Rupert Brooke, handsomer than any movie star. I edit, keeping one eye peeled for the models, straining my ears to hear what they say. In there they photograph the girls on the bamboo furniture, glossies for the pulsing façades of night spots. One day the manager brings me flowers, a huge and damaged bouquet: hurt gladiolas, overly open roses, long-leaping ferns (least hurt), and bruised carnations. I accept the gift, remainder of last night's opening (where?), debut of lower-class blondes. I distribute the flowers in the other poetry rooms, too formal-looking for our disarray.

Now after every model's bow to the footlights the manager brings more flowers, hurt gladiolas, overly open roses, long-leaping ferns and bruised carnations. I edit poems to the click of sharp high heels, flanked by the swords of lavender debut, whiffing the cinnamon of crepe-paper-pink carnations of the bruised and lower-class blondes.

Behind me rears my wall of books, most formidable of human barriers. No flower depresses me like the iris but these I have a fondness for. They bring stale memories over the threshold of the street. They bring the night of cloth palm trees and soft plastic leopard chairs, night of sticky drinks, the shining rhinestone hour in the dark-blue mirror, the peroxide chat of models and photogenic morn.

Today the manager brings all gladioli. A few rose petals lie in the corridor. The mail is heavy this morning.

A Minor Church

The preacher (say Episcopal) alone on a lone day (Tuesday perhaps, off season for great holidays) in his fine small church (not small if you are in it long enough), really in solitude in the minor splendor. One supposes he has finished his chores, whatever they are, and is returning the absorption of the stage-lit solitude. Nevertheless everything is present, with objects having taken on the quality of human beings. He's not what you would call a contemplative. He snatches time like a schoolteacher, or waits for it, miserly, knowing that it will come with interest. And when it comes (which is rather more often than anyone expects, or even wants), his first sensation is collapse, his second to sit where the Sunday people pray. There, though it has the musk of a railroad station (not really), he takes a seat for a moment, gets up, sits down. He is one of them now, in the back of his head. The hedges are such a brown that spring is about to thorn on the world-side of the purple glass with its legends so strictly ruled on the calendar. He has no grief. This paperwork of saving souls! Could there be quiet in the stolen moment, moment of fame with God. But everything stirs, even though noiselessly. Could there be thoughts that turn to stone after the hammering, forever. O leaves of stone, come forth in a cool summering of prayer and change my spirit into a fine small church on the world's quietest street. My hands of vellum folded, I could pray.

Generations

The look of shock on an old friend's face after years of not meeting, as
if perhaps we were in a play, dressed for one of the final acts. The
make-up of the years (infant, schoolboy, lover, soldier, judge of
others, patriarch and ultimate old child) is on us. Those who remain
the same and those who change their jaws. One has milky moons
around the eyes or knotty knuckles. Many and varied are the studies
in gray. The spectrum of whites amazes.

A generation moves in stateliness. It arrives like a pageant and passes down
the street. The children sit on the curbs and watch. There are dig-
nitaries and clowns, the men with medals and the cross-carriers. The
owners walk abreast for the afternoon: they carry the banner which
reads: the business of the world is—business. Manacled dictators
walk alone through the crowded silence: four swordsmen guard them
like points of the compass. The poets arrive on burros, bumping each
other. Theologians packed in a hearse peer out like sickly popes. A
phalanx of technologists singing the latest love songs in marching
rhythms. Movie stars escorting diplomats (it's hard to tell them
apart).

Nine of the greatest novelists, of ridiculous difference in height and girth.
Two modern saints on litters. The generation proceeds to the ceno-
taph, the only common meeting place. In side streets the coming
generation, not even looking, waits its turn and practices a new and
secret language. (They think it's secret: that's what's so depressing.)
Their hero is also gray and still in high school. He drives a hundred
miles an hour into a tree.

Absences

The two-year-old has had a motherless week. Mother has gone to bring back
the baby. A week is many many years. One evening they bring the
news to the playpen: a child is born, you have a baby brother. The
dark little eyes consider this news and convey no message. One day
long after, they arrive in a taxi, father, mother, bundle. The two-year-
old observes from her blue walker on the sunny sidewalk. She stares
and turns away on her wheels.

The father has gone to the other side of the world. He will bring back
strange presents to a strange house. The little ones shyly wait their
turn. Reconciliation is gradual.

In Trenton, New Jersey, the soldiers sit in the innocuous bar. It's three years
since they saw the ones they wrote to. They are all afraid to go home.
One lives two blocks away; he is very silent. Late in the afternoon,
at an ungiven signal, they get up and disperse, like criminals per-
fectly trained for the job ahead.

In my brother's house when I left (whole histories ago) the furniture was
honeymoon fresh, gleam of ceramics; soft beige carpets smelt like
new-mown hay. With a shock I see the carpet is worn; the sofa has
settled; books have changed places. A thousand days of words have
passed.

Time is mostly absences, oceans generally at peace, and lives we love most
often out of reach.

I Am an Atheist
Who Says His Prayers

I am an atheist who says his prayers.

I am an anarchist, and a full professor at that. I take the loyalty oath.

I am a deviate. I fondle and contribute, backscuttle and brown, father of three.

I stand high in the community. My name is in *Who's Who*. People argue about my modesty.

I drink my share and yours and never have enough. I free-load officially and unofficially.

A physical coward, I take on all intellectuals, established poets, popes, rabbis, chiefs of staff.

I am a mystic. I will take an oath that I have seen the Virgin. Under the dry pandanus, to the scratching of kangaroo rats, I achieve psychic onanism. My tree of nerves electrocutes itself.

I uphold the image of America and force my luck. I write my own ticket to oblivion.

I am of the race wrecked by success. The audience brings me news of my death. I write out of boredom, despise solemnity. The wrong reason is good enough for me.

I am of the race of the prematurely desperate. In poverty of comfort I lay gunpowder plots. I lapse my insurance.

I am the Babbitt metal of the future. I never read more than half of a book. But that half I read forever.

I love the palimpsest, statues without heads, fertility dolls of the continent of Mu. I dream prehistory, the invention of dye. The palms of the dancers' hands are vermillion. Their heads oscillate like the cobra. High-caste woman smelling of earth and silk, you can dry my feet with your hair.

I take my place beside the Philistine and unfold my napkin. This afternoon I defend the Marines. I goggle at long cars.

Without compassion I attack the insane. Give them the horsewhip!

The homosexual lectures me brilliantly in the beer booth. I can feel my muscles soften. He smiles at my terror.

Pitchpots flicker in the lemon groves. I gaze down on the plains of Hollywood. My fine tan and my arrogance, my gray hair and my sneakers, O Israel!

Wherever I am I become. The power of entry is with me. In the doctor's office a patient, calm and humiliated. In the foreign movies a native, shabby enough. In the art gallery a person of authority (there's a secret way of approaching a picture. Others move off). The high official insults me to my face. I say nothing and accept the job. He offers me whiskey.

How beautifully I fake! I convince myself with men's room jokes and epigrams. I paint myself into a corner and escape on pulleys of the unknown. Whatever I think at the moment is true. Turn me around in my tracks; I will take your side.

For the rest, I improvise and am not spiteful and water the plants on the cocktail table.

Statue of Liberty

To the poor (aux pauvres) crime alone (le crime seul) opens (ouvre) les
portes de la vie (the doors of life). Entire libraries of music are
hurled in the gutters: the G.I.'s are looking for bottles. The Bavarian
Venus is snatched baldheaded.

I have a big sister; she has mighty breasts. She writes poems for the immigra-
tion office. Her crotch is on the fourteenth floor. La géante, la géante!

Standing at the pure white rail, stately we pass you, and the classes mingle
as if by decree. At the last buoy the discreet signs begin to take
effect: First Class, Second Class. My brazen sister swirling her night-
gown, green as the spouts of Chartres. Her comb is combing my lice
(but I have no lice). Her apron is hitched up in front. She stands on
a full-sized bank.
Across the iambic pentameter of the Atlantic (the pilot dropped, the station
wagon in the hold) we sail to the kingdom of Small. Is it cheaper
there? Can I buy a slave?

Amsterdam Whores

Each in her well-lighted picture window, reading a book or magazine, the Amsterdam whores look quite domestic. The canals, as picturesque as expected, add their serenity. The customers stroll from window to window, back and forth, comparing merchandise. Where a curtain is drawn, business is being transacted. These are big, fine, strapping whores, heavy in the leg, blond, as is the preference. They don't display their wares, no more than crossing a leg. It's like a picture gallery, Flemish School, silent through varnish and glaze. What detail, what realism of texture, what narrative! And look at this masterpiece:

A solid blond sits in her window at an angle. She appears to be looking out, expressionless. Just back of her stands an African king in round white hat and lengthy white embroidered robe of satin, it may be. Behind him stands his servant, very straight. The king's face is a thin and noble ebony. And without looking at either African the whore holds one hand back of her shoulder, feeling the robe of the African king with eloquent fingers, weighing the heft of the silk in her thoughtful hand.

Fever

The Bach *Partitas* saved my life. Floating in fever over Cincinnati, I felt the soft piano hammers sounding my chest, my soul, my balls. Ancient and skillful fingers worked their way—genius of chiropractic, I am uncracked again! Crucified on silk rope ladders that tickle the back of my neck I sail down blazing sea lanes with old poems that disgust me nowadays. I'm not sick enough for a reconciliation. Maybe I'm only malingering. The doctor says through a brandy snifter as big as my head: the virus yes, but somebody is bothering you. He's telling my fortune.

Waves of activity spring from the phonograph: the left-hand figure is deep in my bowels. Yes, there's a student wrecking my work. I'm too much of a coward to kick him out. There's a girl who was burned in a fire; I fear for her sanity. Or a Quaker lady bound for jail; and a jazz musician. I've lost the clue for keeping them together.

They used to call it brain fever or broken heart. Medicine was metaphorical in those days. But one can train a deadly disease to run your affairs while you're away. You adopt it while it is young, shower it with affection, give it the confidence of education.

Stay in bed for a week. Learn the *Partitas*. This music forgives me. Love of simplicity, fear of the obvious, at bottom the dread of being an impostor. Is it ever too late to denounce? The music is playing me—the wrong approach as usual.

Jazz

August Saturday night on the Negro street the trolleys clang and break sweet
dusty smoke. Cars hoot meaningless signals. The air is in a sweat of
Jim Crow gaiety, shopping, milling, rubbing of flesh, five miles of
laughter in white Baltimore. The second floor dance hall has a fa-
mous trumpet. You can't move on the floor, which rolls like waves
and is in actual danger of giving way. The temperature adds to the
frenzy. There is no pause in the jump and scream of the jazz, heat
waves of laughter, untranslatable slang. The dancing is demonic,
terpsichorean. It's like a war of pleasure. It's the joy of work. The
fatigue is its own reward.

Across the street in the corner drug store where whiskey is sold and every
blandishment of skin, a teeming Negress crowds at the perfume
counter, big arms like haunches and bosom practically bare. She
laughs with her friends above the cut-glass bottles with Frenchified
names and recently invented colors. She purchases a sizeable vial of
some green scent, pays green dry money, unstoppers the bottle and
dumps the entire load between her breasts! O glorious act of laughter
in the half-serious bazaar of the Jew-store!

Third Class, Queen Mary

Third Class, *Queen Mary,* late December on the high Atlantic. The storm is fabulous. Seas run to the height of the promenade deck where picture windows are smashed. The ocean frowns like elephant hide and has a texture almost smooth. In the dining room I am sat with Miss Cohen at a table for two. (The English keep races together.) I tell her proudly that this was my troopship. Proudly I describe the Mary in wartime: gray from stem to stern, all ports and windows blacked, the monster zigzagging from Boston to the Sydney Heads. Forty days and forty nights, Key West, Rio, Capetown, south almost to Little America, north to New South Wales. Now it seems quiet and empty, clean and well-kept as a cemetery, even in this great storm.—Ah, this is different, says Miss Cohen: we are paying for this.

We are paying for this!

The server is polite and clean. He tends us in the mighty empty ship. The tablecloth is white, the silver silver. The waiters call me Sir. This voyage I am Sir. I pay.

In the vulgarity of poetic justice, Miss Cohen is knocked from her chair by a skyscraper sea. I visit her in the hospital. She is ugly; I like her. I say to myself, she offended the god of the storm.

Flight from Chicago

Not at all my favorite author, Kipling described Chicago once: the water is the water of the Hooghly, and the air is dirt. And as famous a poet of New England whom I drive to the station: it's a grand city. (*Grand,* a nineteenth-century word.)

Under its permanent umbrella of travail, Chicago swirls in grit. Smuts drift in the sky, penetrate window glass, light on petals of window-box flowers, turning geraniums pansy-black. All is charred, all is furred with dirt, the sky winter and summer streaked like the sky-light of the grandest railroad station, basilicas of practical kings.

But now we take leave forever by car, driving in early morning south, miraculously out from under the soiled umbrella, south and more south in the dead blue winter light, south and west in the snow-light, till the snow rots in Arkansas, then west again, the holy direction.

Far from the Chicago cave, spring comes facing toward summer, such summer as happens only in one place in a given country.

There is a rise (where is it on the map?), on one side America and on the other, California. There you look down on promised advertisements of green come true, green for the eating, money-green, and the rows of the royal palm for welcome, official, frightening. The Californians live in California. The money groves are green. America is a suburb of California et cetera et cetera.

America is Hooghly.

Tahiti 1936

The poet takes the voyage to the New Cytherea. Fifty miles from little
Papeete he and his girl have rented a thatched hut. He says the name
of the district over and over: Taravao, Taravao. The hut is right on
the beach; water laps at the pilings. The whole front opens crazily out
and is propped up by a stake. The roof is pandanus, very brown and
dusty, a house of straw. No sooner have they entered when the poet
grabs up a witch's broom and begins to sweep. The girl hangs batiks
on the wall. There are spiders big as your hand. Frozen with terror
the poet smashes them.

Over the water rises Moorea, blue-mauve with lots of red, as the painter
saw it. The poet sweeps and arranges like a woman. He lays out
books. The hut is ready at last; they lean out of the open wall and
worship the world. They make love on the crunchy bed. Later the
natives bring bananas as a gift. Their movements are slow and peace-
ful, their French is soft and broad. Inside the coral reef the swimming
is perfect. They shop in Papeete. They bank at the Bank of Indo-
China. Everything is exotic, even the nuns. At the Post Office a
crowd of French sailors are arguing grimly. Spain is at war with
itself. It has started today. It is even here.

There is only one movie: *Tabu* by Murnau. The natives return to it like a
church. We go there. It is great like literature.

In Japan

In the second-best hotel in Tokyo the chambermaids are chasing the chamberboys. Laughter tinkles up and down the halls. The elevator girls sing it when they say: ten floor, please; seven floor, please (their faces like gardenias). The cashier's fingers race back and forth over the counting frame.

In the first-best Western-style hotel in Kyoto I describe to the barmaid how to make a Bloody Mary, and am proud. I walk through the fish market with the editor of *The Kenyon Review*. The fishes are displayed like masterpieces. This is more beautiful than the Louvre.

I fall in love with the torii gate, graceful salmon arms, the light rust color. From now on it's my Parthenon. The wooden golden palace floats on its pond. The nightingale floors warn me of my assassins. I sleep like an Oriental.

Zen is on the verge of being discovered. We climb to the famous abstract garden and study the sand designs and the rocks. To my companion I say: how do they fix it without messing it up? He laughs at my westernization.

As for the haiku, you can make it tough. It isn't exactly a valentine, except in the States.

Nebraska

I love Nowhere where the factories die of malnutrition.

I love Nowhere where there are no roads, no rivers, no interesting Indians,

Where history is invented in the History Department and there are no centennials of anything,

Where every tree is planted by hand and has a private tutor.

Where the "parts" have to be ordered and the sky settles all questions,

Where travelers from California bitch at the backwardness and New Yorkers step on the gas in a panic,

Where the grass in winter is gray not brown,

Where the population diminishes.

Here on the boundary of the hired West, equidistant from every tourist office, and the air is washed by distance, here at last there is nothing to recommend.

May no one ever attempt a recommendation; Chicago be as far as Karachi.

Though the warriors come with rockets, may they fall off the trucks.

May the voting be light and the clouds like a cruise and the criminal boredom enter the district of hogs.

I love Nowhere where the human brag is a brag of neither time nor place,

But an elephant house of Smithsonian bones and the white cathedrals of grain,

The feeding-lots in the snow with the steers huddled in symmetrical misery, backs to the sleet,

To beef us up in the Beef State plains, something to look at.

The Cracking-Plant

From the top floor of the Tulsa hotel I gaze at the night beauty of the crack-
ing-plant. Candlelit city of small gas flames by the thousands, what
a lovely anachronism dancing below like an adolescent's dream of
the 1880's, the holy gas redeemed from Baudelaire's mustachioed
curses. Elsewhere are the white lights of the age, but here, like a mil-
lionaire who frowns on electricity, the opulence of flame. Descend-
ing on Rome from the air at night, a similar beauty: the weak Italian
bulbs like faulty rheostats yellowly outline the baroque curves of the
Tiber, the semicircles of the monstrous Vatican, endless broken
parabolas.

The cracking-plant is equally palatial. Those oil men in the silent elevator,
like princes with their voices of natural volume, their soft hats and
their name-drops (like balloons of words in the mouths of caricatures
in political cartoons), men of many mansions. The doors of the
room are mahogany. Through one which adjoins and is locked I hear
the guttural laughter of undress, neither leisurely nor quick, indis-
tinct wording, and all is silent but a woman's moan. Now it rises
like the grip of pain; it is almost loud; it is certainly sincere, like the
pent-up grief of deep relief; now it is round, now vibrant, now it is
scaly as it grows. (Then it steps off into nothingness.)

I stand awed in my stocking-feet and move respectfully toward the window,
as a man in an art gallery moves toward a more distant masterpiece
to avoid the musical chatter of intruders. The cracking-plant sails
on through the delicate Oklahoma night, flying the thousand hot flags
of Laputa.

The Parthenon

There's a Parthenon in Nashville large as life, the only perfect replica.
Greeks resent it probably: it sits flat on the ground, like a plane crash
reconstructed. It's not that famous derelict in space (blasted to bits
by a Venetian general). It's not real marble but the brownish con-
crete has the rusty tinge of the Pentelikon. The brownish yellow
came from the Potomac. The British Government cast these Elgin
marbles.

Stepping from your car beneath the West Pediment, you fall back foot
after foot. It crouches over you, a dark red turmoil, savage, bar-
baric—how can this be! Those columns like piano legs, prototype of
Middle Western banks, and brazen doors the biggest in the world.
Only in the Naos where the goddess is gone (she's never been found,
like Eve) the pallid beauty dawns and spreads like cunningly con-
cealed electric light. The beautiful goddess of ivory and gold, torn
into shreds for dagger grips or crucifixes, has no single worshiper
left on the face of the earth, it says at the close of the guidebook. It
was her temple, then it was a church, then it was a mosque (even
with minaret!). Now it's the temple of art. We buy it and sell it fifty
times a day. It's the warehouse of the spirit, a faulty translation.

You, Morosini, dread doge of Venice, what was it like when you saw the
Explosion? A direct hit if there ever was one! And the Turks
thought Athena would protect their gunpowder.

192

Burlesk

Hart Crane, though handicapped, did well with the burlesk: all but her belly
buried in the floor. Magdalene? Perhaps. In Kansas City I pay my
respects to the dying art. The theater is in ruins, the ticket-taker
only half-conscious. Wine took him long ago. The carpet in the aisle
is ripped; twice I snag my foot. The rank air smells of disinfectant.
All seats are vacant except the first two rows. These are lit up as
in a Rembrandt picture, the glowing center of the operation. I sit
down inches from the drum. It lifts my hair each second it is
smashed. The snare drum hisses and the block clicks. The cymbal
crazes.

She's halfway through, already down to the sash that hangs like a silk
muffler between her buttocks. She gyrates with an expert beat, more
round than sharp. Small-breasted, her nipples glitter with stardust—
some local ordinance. She is very pretty, not what you would ex-
pect, almost indifferently dancing her career. Cold flows from her
steady limbs; stately she spreads her thighs for the climactic grind,
when at the highest throw she slips her final string, holding one
hand over the part like a live fig leaf, and flittering her fingers off
—and we are there, and she is all but hairless.

Our faces light up with intelligence.

A Nunnery

Broken bottles hard-set in cement, green glass, brown glass, wavy white and blue, they glitter down the street like distant peaks. I call it St. Mary's of the broken bottle necks. It's the black belt of the town and the old convent. The mossy wall surmounted with jags and hates of glass, hard-set in cement, ledges of rotten ice, yet feminine.

When the sun strikes these fragments like stained glass, what do the sisters feel who walk within these walls? Here are no pictured saints leaded together from the days of blood. Here are the ugly claws of chastity, the long fingernails of theological grief, the severed tendons, castrations for all these perpetually mourning virgins, those lovely Héloïses awakened by knives, deliciously composing love letters forever.

Who drank from these bottles, cracked them so carefully and fixed them in the brick?

In a fine Connecticut living room I saw a Calder once of broken bottles strung in an empty frame. The necks hung free, turning slightly on their slender wires.

Bouquet

All tropic places smell of mold. A letter from Karachi smells of mold. A book I had in New Guinea twenty years ago smells of mold. Cities in India smell of mold and dung. After a while you begin to like it. The curry dishes in the fine Bombay restaurant add the dung flavor. In the villages dung patties plastered to the walls, the leaving of the cows the only cooking fuel. The smell rubs into the blood.

Paris in the winter smells of wood smoke and fruit. Near the Gare St. Lazare in the freezing dusk the crowds pour slowly down the streets in every direction. A police van the size of a Pullman car goes at a walking pace. The gendarme keeps jumping down from the rear like a streetcar conductor in the old days. He is examining identity cards of pedestrians, especially the females. A girl comes swinging along, her pocketbook in rhythm with her behind. She is bareheaded and wears a raincoat. The gendarme examines her identity card. She is motioned into the paddy wagon.

Salzburg, the castle smells of snow and peat. Baltimore, old oaken bucket. Portsmouth, Virginia, roses and diesel oil. Dublin, coal dust, saccharine whiskey, bitter bodies. Damp gusts of Siena doorways. Warehouses of Papeete, acrid smell of copra, frangipani, salt water and mold. Smell of rotting water in Hollandia.

Unbreathable jungles, parks subtle and cool. Backstage the ballet dancers wipe their sweat; "the entire stage stinks like a stable." Sewer gas of beauty parlors. Electric smell of hair in rut. Talcum powder, earliest recollection. Rome, the armpit of the universe.

California/Italy

Italy spoiled California for me. California spoiled Italy. Now I'm back in
the Middle West, where I don't really belong. Nor can I go back
East. Living in that Etruscan pine forest, maddened by too much sun,
I watched the clouds gather up where Siena would be, and no rain
came. Admittedly, it was the drying season. Heat of Florence on a
Sunday afternoon. The horse almost fainted, pulling six in a buggy.
Floods at Christmas in the Sacramento Valley: camellias floating in
the gutters. The final fakery of palm trees in the palm-tree countries:
emblem of grandiose injustice. In Nebraska the Russian olive, fruit-
less. Drunken smell of pine between Fredericksburg and Richmond
and atop the Donner Pass. In Italy the scent barely perceptible, the
bland Mediterranean, reddish yolks of eggs and dirty shells. The
large soft Californians sideswiping the future: the small burning Ital-
ians endlessly plotting nothing. Everywhere the competition of boast-
ing. Only the Navajo questioning time: what is a year? he asks. Does
it have arms and legs? In Baltimore, walking in Victorian-movie
snow it occurred to me: seek for the opposite. I'm for the Faustian
supermarket. The opposite enthralls me. I refuse the wine of the
locale. I smash customs like crockery. The Minnesota accent is
music to my ears. The New Yorker is talking to me at top speed;
the Frenchwoman flies into the conversation at breakneck; I slow
them down with extreme modesty. Always at heart a central Cali-
fornian, I nurse my own geography, miles of tomatoes, tons of sugar
beets. I call a farm a ranch. But no palm trees.

The Magi

Oriental, you give and give. No Christian ever gave like you. What is it you are giving morning and night, asking nothing in return? Pearls, silk cloths, books and scrolls, mother-of-pearl chopsticks, bronze cowbells, hand-painted poetry, tributes of every description. Flowers around my neck, morning, noon, and night: I am ready to vomit. You lay all Asia at my feet—where is your modern sense of values? You're not like a Frenchman, who gives as an investment. Not like an American whose gifts fall out of his pocket. Your gifts are permanent, an end in themselves. We'll cure you yet.

A rope of jasmine flowers round my neck at the airport, the embarrassing bow, the immaculate dark men come with their cargo. The frenzied Westerner grabs it all, the powder barrel stowed under the high altar, in case. The wise men continue to give: a sack of spices for the rotten meat of English queens; antimacassars; Zen.

It's as if you said, that's all I have to give, namely, the works. You never say, leave us alone. That's Western talk. You say, come for a swim in the old sky: my eyes are upside down. You say, the turtle can draw in its legs; the seer can draw in his senses; I call him illumined. In India eyes are never wide open. I throw a bucket of cold water over your continent. Get up from your bed of nails, you wise men of the East. I'm giving you a power plant for Christmas.

Ramakrishna

The rice around the lingam stone will be distributed in the dying sun to the unblessed poor. I bring neither rice nor overpowering jasmine but only my full gaze of love and loathing. With the beautiful Hindu woman I drink in the phallus. On her face the trace of a sneer. (She may be Christian.) Under the nine domes of the Kali temple we make our way to the Divine Mother, Savior of the Universe, Kali in basalt, in gold and precious stones. She stands on Siva. A garland of skulls hangs from her neck. In one of her four hands a severed human head; with another she gives the sign of peace. Her triple eyes bring peace or terror. This was Ramakrishna's darling, standing on Siva, who lies supine on the thousand-petaled silver-lotus.

He drank her smile till all was blue, that saint. He joined the hands of all the gods. In his room a picture of Christ as well. He reached the seventh plane at will.

High Cheekbones

This Slavic typist had high cheekbones and gigantic mouth and a voice like sleep. That Kyoto hostess naturally. Marlene, Medea, and my wife, women proud as Tartars, women with marvelous voices and big feet have high cheekbones and dress their hair to a height. In overcivilized rooms you will always find one or two.

The Victorian houri had an oval face, a drooping silkiness of flesh like ottomans. She melted away in the dawn of the century. A drunken poet roars out across the room: are you a tit man or an ass man? I mumble in reply: high cheekbones.

Verlaine compares the buttocks and the breasts: buttocks the holy throne of the indecencies. Breasts savored by drunken lips and the tongue. Buttocks with their ravine of rose and somber shadow, where desire prowls when it goes crazy. Breasts proud and victorious, breasts heavy and powerful. Buttocks, beloved cushions, with a voluptuous fold for your face or your sex. O holy quaternity of sacred breasts and august buttocks.

Poets with high cheekbones, Rimbaud, Pasternak.

Adultery

Hymen's got a cold. Hymen, your nose is running.

My love, you look like Beethoven, like you were hit by a truck.
You look like a fucking skull.

It's six o'clock, you're drunk, you speak Greek in your sleep, you snore like
   Henry the Ninth. Wake up and take the dimes off my eyes.

The head of shame is red. The revenue stamp on the liquor bottle is red.
   Accidental baby, where's the Med School?

Trafe is the color of my true love's hair. Thank God for rain, blizzards,
   onions, and clap. Head like a broken sunflower rolling on its neck.

Coat, I place my hands in your empty pockets, thievery of nihilo, all the
   same illegal. Hands are illegal, teeth and tongue, books, bottles,
   dry rust carnations, babies, weeping, and law.

Two cars, one male, one female in every nest of love.

Two hearts with internal combustion engines.

Moving Day

Sorrow has moved away like happiness. The **Bros.** depart.

When poetry is written the trucks come. The Bros. are here. China is being packed in Cheerio cartons, the best books are wrapped in Dacron drawers. The Bros. are careful.

Great vans that smash vacationers like cockroaches, vans with names as high as windmills, noble, impersonal.

End in sight, I have your phone number. I make the nasty clicks of the dial, quickly, with the accuracy of the drum of an empty revolver. Sounds fall, like when the pussy willow goes to seed, or heady dandelions or sycamore trash balls.

Ex stasis—out of this world. Teamsters Union.

The song of the phone has quit. To kalon, to kakon.

The clock-radio is still, la mauvaise foi. What! Is it nothing but that?

Night. The sky is torn and ripped, creating panic in the eye of the beholder. Few look up. The van sits in the duende darkness with the admirable stupidity of officials.

And sleeping beauty Nihilo lies sleeping.

After the War

After a war the boys play soldier with real weapons. This is a real hand grenade, a pineapple. The killing stuff has been removed but the pin remains to pull out and push in. There is a clip to hang it from your belt. The pineapple is a red-brown iron the color of—a pineapple, very heavy to hold, very heavy to throw, though small. All the boys own a pineapple. The squares are cut deep in the metal fruit. When it explodes, we say, you have diced pineapple and dying men and a hole in the ground.

The dummy rifles are dark-brown wood. Every part is round and smooth. There is no metal, no trigger assembly. The dummy muzzle comes to a rubber end like a truncheon or a heavy walking stick. It is five feet tall and too heavy for boys to hold out straight in the standing position, but fine to hold prone or stand in the corner of the bedroom.

The shallow helmet is rough to the feel, a greenish basin with a cocky steel brim. Inside, the webbing is leather to fit the skull and carry the shock. Mine has a handsome dent in the top, a round dent with a crease at the bottom. There is a delicate line of rust in the crease, a close call for somebody.

Today we play on the gray wooden battleship built on the grass for the sailors' drills. This must be the biggest toy in the world, a full-sized ship, a ship out of water, all above ground, without a keel. The Naval Base is always open to boys. The Naval Base is filled with flowered walks and neat straight lines and whitewashed curbs. The officers' houses are white and face the Bay. The wooden battleship is a school. It never rocks but runs up fluttering flags. The ship browses at peace among the flowers of the Naval Base. The Shore Police in their sentry boxes at the main entrance don't even notice us as we come and go. We are part of the game.

The shell-shocked newsman stomps down Granby Street, shouting commands and thumping his truncheon-stick on the ground. Nobody laughs at him; everyone says he is harmless. The fits of stomping and shouting commands come once or twice a day. Then he subsides in a truce with himself. When there are parades he stands at attention.

Leaving the troopship, men hacked at walls, slit mattresses, broke pipes, gouged at lounge-room ornamentation, middle-class British taste for luxury liners, made minor desecrations of the great gray leviathan. On this voyage of forty days and forty nights the Americans consumed a quarter of a million Coca-Colas, the sergeant says, and spits between his feet.

The General returns with the power of a god. His disgrace is a triumph. The world pours at his feet like a tide; it swirls through cities and engulfs skyscrapers. Men become frightened at their own frenzy. In Chicago the cheering and weeping are endemic, maniacal. The General is handsome, arrogant, and wrong. Such a General might be the President. He leaves his car to lay a wreath on a bridge across the poisonous Chicago River. He delivers his profile to rich and poor. In the war his communiqués always mentioned God. We hated him.

Fox Hole

Quintana lay in the shallow grave of coral. The guns boomed stupidly fifty yards away. The plasma trickled into his arm. Naked and filthy, covered with mosquitoes, he looked at me as I read his white cloth tag. How do you feel, Quintana? He looks away from my gaze. I lie: we'll get you out of here sometime today.

I never saw him again, dead or alive. Skin and bones, with eyes as soft as soot, neck long as a thigh, a cross on his breastbone not far from the dog tags. El Greco was all I could think of. Quintana lying in his shallow foxhole waiting to be evacuated. A dying man with a Spanish name equals El Greco. A truck driver from Dallas probably.

When the Japs were making the banzai charge, to add insult to death, they came at us screaming the supreme insult: *Babe Ruth, go to hell!* The Americans, on the other hand, when the Japs flew over dropping sticks of explosives, shouted into the air, as if they could hear: *Tojo, eat shit!*

Soldiers fall in love with the enemy all too easily. It's the allies they hate. Every war is its own excuse. That's why they're all surrounded with ideals. That's why they're all crusades.

The Missal

Priests and Freudians will understand. In the throttling Papuan heat, even the rain is hot, even the rain carries the rot smell. Lying in mud or in soaked hammocks the soldiers stew and joke and empty their dead minds. Deprived of love and letters and the sight of woman, the dead mind rots.

Who sent this missal soft and black, with iridescent gold and five silk ribbons sewn in the binding: red, silver, blue, green, purple? Two thousand pages mica-thin, like two millennia of daily shame.

Nearby, the natives make themselves strong by drinking sweat of warriors, eating fingernails coated with human blood. Priests and Freudians comprehend. And now I learn the missal prayers. I set up mental prayer wheels and spin them with the whips of fear. Help me, Freudians and priests: when I say the proud Hail Mary, the serpent takes me in the groin.

I seek the chaplain in his tent. Father, convert me. He looks at me and says: You must excuse me, sergeant. I have a furlough coming up.

When I say the Hail Mary I get an erection. Doesn't that prove the existence of God?

Lower the Standard

Lower the standard: that's my motto. Somebody is always putting the food out of reach. We're tired of falling off ladders. Who says a child can't paint? A pro is somebody who does it for money. Lower the standards. Let's all play poetry. Down with ideals, flags, convention buttons, morals, the scrambled eggs on the admiral's hat. I'm talking sense. Lower the standards. Sabotage the stylistic approach. Let weeds grow in the subdivision. Putty up the incisions in the library façade, those names that frighten grade-school teachers, those names whose U's are cut like V's. Burn the *Syntopicon* and *The Harvard Classics*. Lower the standard on classics, battleships, Russian ballet, national anthems (but they're low enough). Break through to the bottom. Be natural as an American abroad who knows no language, not even American. Keelhaul the poets in the vestry chairs. Renovate the Abbey of cold-storage dreamers. Get off the Culture Wagon. Learn how to walk the way you want. Slump your shoulders, stick your belly out, arms all over the table. How many generations will this take? Don't think about it, just make a start. (You have made a start.) Don't break anything you can step around, *but don't pick it up*. The law of gravity is the law of art. You first, poetry second, the good, the beautiful, the true come last. As the lad said: We must love one another or die.

Seed Catalogs

Why poetry small and cramped, why poetry starved and mean, thin-lipped
and sunken-cheeked? Why these pams, these narrow-shouldered neg-
atives? (The best we can say is that they're seed catalogs.) And why
those staring eyes, so carefully fixed on the photographic plate? Why
no lips at all but in their stead the practiced line of anger and the
clamped jaw? Why always the darkening halo, so seemingly satanic?
(The best we can say is that they are trying to mirror our lives.
Do they know our lives? Can they read past the symbols of our
trade?) Why so much attention to the printed page, why the cos-
metology of font and rule, meters laid on like fingernail enamel?
Why these lisping indentations, Spanish question marks upside
down? Why the attractive packaging of stanza? Those cartons so
pretty, shall I open them up? Why the un-American-activity of the
sonnet? Why must grown people listen to rhyme? How much longer
the polite applause, the tickle in the throat?

What will fatten you, skinny little book? What will put lead in your pencil?
All of you dust-collecting seed catalogs, to the Goodwill you go, to
the broad stench of the paper mill! Seed catalog, go pulp yourself!

Poems, flowers of language, if that's what you are, grow up in the air
where books come true. And you, thin packet, let your seed fly,
if you have any.

The Nature of Belief

When suffering is everywhere, that is of the nature of belief. When the leaders are corrupted, Pope or Commissar, nor do the people flicker an eyelash, that is of the nature of belief. When there are anniversaries of battle or martyrdom, that is of the nature of belief. When there is the slogan Credo quia absurdum or intellectual proof of the existence of God, that is of the nature of belief. When priests pray for victory and generals invoke heaven, when prisons fill with children, that is of the nature of belief. When the word *evil* appears in newspapers, *moral* in the mouths of policemen, *culture* in the prepared speeches of politicians, all that is of the nature of belief. Belief makes blood flow. Belief infects the dead with more belief. Now it flows in our veins. Now it floats in the clouds.

Libraries

Libraries, where one takes on the smell of books, stale and attractive. Service with no motive, simple as U.S. Mail. Fountains and palms, armchairs for smokers. Incredible library where ideas run for safety, place of rebirth of forgotten anthems, modern cathedral for lovers. Library, hotel lobby for the unemployed, the failure, the boy afraid to go home, penniless. Switchboards for questioners: What do you know about unicorns? How do you address a duchess? Palladian architecture of gleaming glass and redwood. Window displays of this week's twelve best-sellers. Magnificent quarters of the director, who dines with names of unknown fame. Lavatories, rendezvous of desperate homosexuals. In the periodical room the newspapers bound with a stick, carried like banners of surrender to pale oak tables. Library, asylum, platform for uninhibited leaps. In the genealogy room the delicate perspiration of effete brains. Room also of the secret catalogue, room of unlisted books, those sought by police, manuscript room with the door of black steel, manuscripts stolen in delicate professional theft from abroad, sealed for seventy-five years. Sutras on spools of film. And all this courtesy and all this trust, tons of trash and tons of greatness, burning in time with the slow cool burning, burning in the fires of poems that gut libraries, only to rebuild them, more grand and Palladian, freer, more courteous, with cornerstones that say: Decide for yourself.

French Poetry

French poetry that always goes itself one better.

French poetry of figure 5's and rust carnations.

French poetry of the tongue that tastes of women and children, spatulas and rubber plants.

French poetry of the tiniest print to be read with bifocals when snow first enters the rain with its wicked announcements of defeat.

French poetry of marginal headaches, wood fires, cold, sixteen-millimeter surrealist films, Martinique jazz and the woman across the way, utmost gravity and indestructible balance, winner of the double medallion,

Easter Island images, the monstrous solemnity of patriotic children and ribbons.

French poetry of convenience, Satanism, baroque brass keys to hospitals, and cats.

French poetry of the line drawn with the fist on the pale nuance,

Overly cultivated snows, sick castles.

French poetry of the exquisite ruins of conversation.

French poetry that upsets the stomach of the future.

Of frockless priests, glorious geometricians, child insurrectionists.

French poetry of the Statue of Liberty, battered by kisses and dentists,

Ropy veins of the feet of matrons and whores, stigmata, épée.

French poetry of the Missouri River, the Platte, Yarra, gutter water of the rue Jacob.

Gloire, Vrai, et cetera.

Baudelaire in Iowa

They held a celebration for you, Charles, in Iowa. I was asked but I
regretted. It was the hundredth birthday of your book, your proper
Christian book called *Flowers of Evil*. (Or is it THE *Flowers of Evil?*
I never know.) And in that hymnal, how well you made yourself in
the image of Poe—Poe with a cross, that's what you are, adored
of the gangster age. In fact, aren't you a children's poet? Aren't you
the Lewis Carroll of small vice? Your shabby Wonderland of pus and
giant nipple, your cats and jewels and cheap perfumes, your licking
Lesbians and make-believe Black Mass, O purulence of Original Sin.
And always playing it safe in the end, like Disneyland. So many safety
devices, pulleys, cranks, classical Alexandrines. It's Iowa for you,
restless spirit, where elderly ladies embezzle millions in the *acte
gratuite*. You'll need no naturalization papers here. And yet I loved
you once, and Delacroix and Berlioz—all in my gangster age. The
little boy in me loved you all, O solemn Charles, so photogenic. And
this is my flower for your anniversary. I fashioned it of Mexican tin
and black nail polish, little French Swinburne burning in Iowa City.

Randall Jarrell

Randall, I like your poetry terribly, yet I'm afraid to say so. Not that my praise keeps you awake—though I'm afraid it does. I can't help liking them. I even like the whine, the make-believe whiplash with the actual wire in it. Once when you reviewed me badly (you must) I wrote you: "I felt as if I had been run over but not hurt." That made you laugh. I was happy. It wasn't much of a triumph but it worked. When people ask about you I am inclined to say: He's an assassin (a word I never use). I'm inclined to say: Why are you always yourself? Your love of Rilke—if it's love—your intimacy with German and God knows what all, your tenderness and terrorization, your prose sentences—like Bernini graves, staggeringly expensive, Italianate, warm, sentences once-and-for-all. And the verses you leave half-finished in mid-air—I once knew a woman who never finished a sentence. Your mind is always· at its best, your craft the finest craft "money can buy" you would say with a barb. I'm afraid of you. Who wouldn't be. But I rush to read you, whatever you print. That's news.

Wilhelm Reich

I drove three thousand miles to ask a question. No answer, naturally. It served me right; I'm not the pilgrim type. I wanted a first-hand account of *him:* when he was alive, before they murdered him. When you worked with him, before they drove him insane, I laughed like the others. I said: My friend, you swim among the blues of the lunatic fringe as always. This is only another of your voyages. But did you leave him before he died or after? Did you go to the trial? Were you there when the police smashed the equipment? Did you visit him in the sunset of his mind?

In the soft San Diego sunset you turned your back. I don't want to talk about that, you said. Your little dogs leaped up at me with teeth. Our children ran wild together. Your wife sang beautifully. In the morning you cashed me a check, arriving at the bank in a foreign car.

Did you really recover from the death of your father? I must hear about the other from someone I know as well as you. You are the only one. We didn't get along was all you said. I don't want to discuss him. The disciples are scattered. They are all in hiding. It's against the law to post his books. Everyone seems ashamed for a different reason. Is his wife living, his child? Where is truth's underground? How long does love stay murdered? Did he have to sentence himself? The lab experiment of his life is proved—there must have been another way. Pictures that he took when the bulbs popped, each brighter than a thousand suns; the spiral poems he wrote under the electronic microscope—mad scientist, good German—fixed in my mind and locked in yours.

Caitlin Thomas

Cat called me a Jewish pig. Cat said to me in a voice so normal she might
 be ordering ham from a yard-high menu: You are the most insensi-
 tive man I've ever met.

Cat and I were walking down the Cathouse street off Bughouse Square in
 Chicago. Her husband was trying to lose us (you can hardly
 blame him). Where is your lovely husband, Cat? She wheeled around
 and pointed through the neon baleful glare: There comes the little
 fucker, that little black thing two inches high.

She sulked on a sofa in a shabby dress, looking like an Irish maid on her
 day off in the walnut-paneled living room. She seethed with worms
 at so much rich stupidity. Hell flowed from her mouth like streams of
 horse, splashing the blue Picassos.

For breakfast we have beer. Where the scum of fame backed up in the
 estuary Cat bathed with hopeless soap. The sky grew dingier than
 pans. In the vomit of news she spun like a carousel and fell
 through sobs to the dromedary dolls.

Cat went walking through the slaughterhouse where the prime hogs dance
 on the end of a chain and the throats are slit to empty the black
 blood. She groaned in the screaming of pork and was given per-
 fume.

Cat left her laundry and forgot to get it. Five miles in the air you could
 hear her scream of love. At the soup kitchen of poets she gloomed
 like a sphinx. She stroked the oxygen tank like a bomb with a name.
 She exhausted the language of blame. With the dry shrapnel of
 love she shaved her head in the gleaming sleet of literature. Her
 typewriter keys were tipped with tetanus praise. She cursed the
 cyclamen, good Saint Cat.

Clowning

Dylan wasn't dapper. Uncle Saul was a dandy. Dylan stole and borrowed. Uncle Saul likewise. Dylan stole a shirt or two and some bottles of whiskey. Uncle Saul purloined whole wardrobes, used checking accounts that didn't belong to him, charged at the best shops under others' names. Dylan wore motley, Uncle Saul silk. Dylan was short and curly. Uncle Saul wore Cuban heels to raise himself and ordered Scotch in the barber's chair. Dylan played at pinballs. Uncle won the monthly rent at poker or bridge. Dylan borrowed women. Uncle Saul hired them and kept them in love nests. Dylan's look was straight and far into your eyes. The eyes of Uncle Saul were always merry and shrewd but you couldn't see beyond their twinkle and scheme. Dylan was a civilian. Uncle wangled a commission in the Army, only to be discharged for juggling money records. Uncle Saul kept the table choking with laughter and sang falsetto and clowned in a lavender dressing gown, with masses of hair on his chest. Dylan toured America like a favorite nephew, sprinkling dynamite on the nipples of female professors. He had the discipline of a lovely knave.

Now both are dead, Dylan and Uncle Saul. Dylan was taken by the pickling of his beautiful brain. The sacred oxygen could not reach the convolutions. Uncle Saul was taken thrice by the heart, thrice by the broken personality. Uncle Saul joked in the lobby of the plush nuthouse, wearing a brilliant sportcoat and shined elegant shoes. The black hair dye had vanished; his hair was snowy white. They gave him the shock treatment until his heart exploded. Dylan lay inert with the Moses bumps on his forehead amidst the screaming of wives and the groans of lovers and drinkers. And the Beat said—iambic killed him.

Henry Miller

He said it: Kill the poet in yourself. He said it well. Now he is surrounded
by juries in every direction. Whole passages are read by the court
clerk; the women bow their heads as if in prayer. Some have never
even heard the words that kill. The men are always angriest or ag-
grieved. I think: the pig is taboo to the Jews bceause it was once their
god. Are those words gods? The people want their poetry of not
saying, don't touch, hold your shoulders straight. They turn the book
in their hands like a time bomb. Something goes off in their laps
but no one is frightened. Much talk of taking a bath. A bidet is
brought for exhibit. Demonstrations. Laughter. Waving of state flags.
No one is certain precisely what the issue is. The testimony grows
learned; big words are rolled in like balls of dung. Why are the edges
of the Bible red not blue? I think we are losing. The experts falter.
Housewives examine their fingernails: this is the end. The hilarious
thing is the way he sides with the judges, like Jesus. The veil is rent
by a tremendous blat. Dogs cry in their sleep. Children playing
doctor are hustled off to the federal prisons. The wife of the Presi-
dent crosses herself before releasing the bottle of champagne against
the lead wall of the fall-out shelter. The judge is clutching the Good.
Nobody knows what happened to the True. The Beautiful has fainted
dead away (she has her instructions).

Homo Poet

The day you discover that your favorite poet is a homosexual, and the
heated argument dies down after an hour, and you have lost, you
are like a prince who has been brought bad tidings and you sit with
an empty belly while they take the messenger out of the room to be
shot. Tomorrow it will be different but tonight you feel an imper-
sonal sorrow as nagging as envy. When later you read his poems,
with another dimension added to their music, they will seem more
distant, like fine translations. A dry wash of the face will suffice for
your pleasure. It's not the same as with Shakespeare or the plain
Cavafy. You can shrug at the Greeks and the Bulgarians. But this
is a secret that had to be told to be known.

Close the door of your mind on those love letters. Beware of the poison
of pronouns. Suddenly you are coarse with limitation, gruff before
flowers, your own poems lumpy, indelicate. The it-ness of trees! And
Emily too? And the brotherhood of man—is that one? Penitentiaries,
navies, hospitals, football teams! Where will it end?

Poet who lies with the sea, dancer who shrugs one shoulder, lecturer with
the turquoise ring, exquisite conversationalist, you with the beard
and the lake-water eyes, woman with the voice of woodwinds—why
do you slap me? Is there a poetry where what happens in bed is lucky
on the page and the poem is actually for her?

Roethke

Glottal as a bottle, everybody loves you, only you don't believe it. Hulk
of greenery among the desert great, your roots grab continents of
sham and groan. You masticate all dictionaries and spew out one-
word spitballs on the walls. You blackboard buccaneers of blah.
You housel planetaria of spurt. You shoeshine flesh with hail and
hurt. Psychologically, you sport.

The music flutes: you're nursing Mother Goose. You know her nasty secrets
like a name (dirty old woman stinking of gin). Have you found the
pickled foetuses! Does your poem purl in Polish? Who's bigger than
you—those squishy dreams?   •

The decencies file in: such pretty girls, such beardy boys. Your rhythms that
throb like ocean motors.

Now and then the darkness of stanzas. That bridge of ice-capped sawtooth
monuments bites at the sky like industrial diamonds. You grit your
teeth on broken glass, sing with a geographical tongue on the sly
nights of Seattle. Art is a blood pudding foreign as frescoes. Where
you dig down we are, we are. Under the smoky glass we are. How
the flukes splash, ha-ha, baby!

Prosody

Why am I happy writing this textbook? What sublime idiocy! What a waste of time! A textbook on prosody at that. Yet when I sit down to comb the business out, when I address the easel of this task, I burn with an even flame, I'm cooking with gas. There are some things so dull they hypnotize like the pendulum of a clock; so clockwork and quotidian they make the flesh delirious like fresh water. X-ray the poem, give it a thorough physical, a clean bill of health. We can see everything but the flow of blood. What Latin and Greek nomenclature! But this is order, order made to order. This is system to plot and plan. This is definition, edges clean as razors. Simplification, boldface, indented. I know there is no such thing as a textbook. I know that all textbooks are sold the second the course is over. I know that a book sold is a dead book. And I dream, like others, of writing a textbook that is not a textbook, a book that not even a student would part with, a book that makes even prosody breathe. So, when the sun shines with the nine o'clock brightness and the coffee swims in my throat and the smoke floats over the page like the smoke of a ship's funnel, then I romanticize. I make a muse of prosody, old hag. She's just a registered nurse, I know, I know, but I have her sashay, grind and bump, register Alcaics, Sapphics, choriambs (my predilection). She's trained all right. She's second nature herself. She knows her job, I mine. We'll work it out: it may be poetry. Blueprints are blue. They have their dreams.

Poets' Corner

As richly documented as the hell of priests, yes, there is a hell, the hell of
   sick poets, the hell of history. Those in whom honesty has turned to
   policy. Those diseased by notice. Those who invent new prosodies,
   with a logical or graphic notation. Those who wear the cold hand-
   cuffs of rhyme. Those who construct a religion of the beautiful, with
   symbols as the means and myth as the end. Those who mistake rage
   for intensity, symmetry for design, metaphor for focus, drunkenness
   for vision. Those who make an example of their lives and who com-
   mit acts of personal violence for public response. These inhabit the
   hell of poets.

Some die early by disease or accident. Some jump in the sea or drink
   lacerating poisons manufactured for toilets. Some lie in asylums with
   eyeballs metamorphosed to marble. (You cannot penetrate below
   their surface.) Some fall on their knees before two pieces of wood or
   a stone belly. Some join the revolutions and are gladly shot. Some
   become officials, laureates, men of affairs or major diplomats. Some
   become abstractionists, actuaries, mathematicians. Some become
   salesmen or lay priests, after their voluptuous poems are in print.
   Some become preachers in the last half of their lives, constructing
   faultless sermons. Some succumb to pageantry, some to algolagnia.

The Bust

They erect a bust of me after my death. I know the right alcove, where
the students sit, in the library corridor, smoking and joking about
the professors. "I fought with tooth and nail to save my niche."

A bust in the modern mode, more than slightly abstract, in a dull metal
perhaps, of the new alloys I love. No lapis lazuli "big as a Jew's
head cut off at the nape." I wish I had a leonine head, the kind to
start a sculptor's fingers twitching.

There was a bust of me a student made, life-size and a good likeness,
age twenty-one when I wore a pompadour. In plaster it was much
too white. We painted it green, then pink, then black, then sand-
papered it down and called it Scrofula. One night we stuck it in a
mound of dirt outside where they were mending the street. That
was the end of it. Baltimore has too many monuments already.

Baltimore has Poe and also Lanier. Lizette Reese and Francis Scott Key.
Baltimore has poets and poets. —Which uncle put the money up?

Esthetics

What the analyst said when he came from the exhibit (he was rather drunk) amounted to this: A clean white wall in an uncluttered room is the ground. You take a clean white wall and hang a rock, a sock, a split of log, a bag of dreck—give it the frame of a clean white wall, and that's abstract.

I looked around the clean white room. Schwitters fritterings of old bus tickets, gracefully mounted bit on bit, for fade of color, take of depth, alone on its panel. Bronze drip of narrow stems of bronze Giacometti; teakwood base. Enormous almost idiot head of Christ, hydrocephalic, brushed in dusty yellows. A female thigh, reddish close-grained jarrah wood, with a high polish.

I love abandoned barns weathered to silver, the drip of rust from reinforcement iron stars on old American brick; driftwood of course; objects found to hand; fondling-stones; packets of Japanese black pebbles; shards; undressed planking; ax marks on a fashionable mantle, twelve by twelve; pock-marked travertine; rose-red hinges; ten-cent-store utensils; comic strips with parentheses denoting frustration or beating wings; Samuel Greenberg and Rupert Brooke.

Glad Hand

I'm writing this poem for someone to see when I'm not looking. This is an open book. I want to be careful to startle you gently. The poem is about your looking at it, as one looks at a woman covertly. (I wonder what she's doing in this town; it's a long way from the look in her eyes.) The rings of my big notebook stand open like the rib cage of a baracuda. Careful with your fingers.

I'm writing this poem for an after-dinner friend who's using my pipe tobacco or my pen. I'd like some phrase to catch his eye. I'd like some phrase to wake him up in the early hours, as one wakes up with a fragment of tune in his head (the melody for the day). The toilet bowls glow graciously and there's a box of the best Kleenex on the sink. I'm writing this poem for hospitality. I can't stand people who say Help Yourself. That always means Don't Be a Pig. Tired of picking the locks of poems I leave this one for all and sundry. To put your name in it would be a dirty trick.

Younger I dreamed of being a poet whose trash basket was rifled by scholars. I learned to write trash-basket poems. But this is closer to my real desire. I'm writing this poem as much for you as a poem is possible. It stands there like a half-filled glass, both coming and going. I'm a bad host. The drinks are too strong; I don't know how to carve (I say with a grin, I'm left-handed). This is a poem to sneak at a glance. (I'm writing it to mean, not be.)

Fame

What kind of notation is in my *Time* file for my life, especially my death?
Will they say I died, O God? If they don't say I died how can I die?
There it is fine and relevant to die, an honor so to speak, interesting as divorce.

What's in my file at the F.B.I.? What's my symbol when they flick me out?
Am I a good American or a borderline case? Can I hold my liquor?
Have I ever been cleared, and if so, of what?

Dear Fame, I meet you in the damnedest places. You smile, you walleyed
bitch, but you look over my shoulder for a prearranged signal:
something has come up on the other side of the room.

My life, my own, who is writing you on what pale punch cards? Deep-
thinking machine, have you got my number?

A hundred oligarchs in identical suits are sitting around a table shaped like
a uterus, alphabetizing greatness. I say to myself: all men are great.
I would like to cry but have forgotten how. Now I remember: they
used to come to me, those journalists with humble pencils. They
begged me from their hats: say something big; give us an execu-
tion; make bad weather. I failed them badly. I couldn't grow a
beard.

I guess I haven't built my ship of death. The word "image" is now in govern-
ment. The doors are all closing by remote control. But when I meet
the almighty Publicity Director, name-dropper of kings, I'll shake
his hand and say: once I kissed Fame (mouth like an ass hole) but
only for fun. He'll tear up the punch cards and think for a
minute.

The Funeral of Poetry

The password of the twentieth century: Communications (as if we had to invent them). Animals and cannibals have communications; birds and bees and even a few human creatures called artists (generally held to be insane). But the bulk of humanity had to invent Communications. The Romans had the best roads in the world, but had nothing to communicate over them except other Romans. Americans have conquered world-time and world-space and chat with the four corners of the earth at breakfast. The entire solar system is in the hands of cartoonists.

I am sitting in the kitchen in Nebraska and watching a shrouded woman amble down the market in Karachi. She is going to get her morning smallpox shot. It's cold and mental love they want. It's the mystic sexuality of Communications. The girl hugs the hi-fi speaker to her belly: it pours into her openings like gravy. Money was love. Power was love. Communications now are love. In the spring Hitler arises. This is the time of trampling.

A man appears at the corner of the street; I prepare myself for hospitality. Man or angel, welcome! But I am afraid and double-lock the door. On the occasion of the death of a political party, I send an epitaph by Western Union. I didn't go to the funeral of poetry. I stayed home and watched it on television.

from
The
Place
of
Love

Bath-Sheba

And I will yet be more vile than thus, and will be base in mine own sight: and of the maidservants which thou hast spoken of, of them shall I be had in honor.

1

And it came to pass in the evening
When the heat melts in the sky like lead
And the breeze comes from Baal-Hamon,
King David rose from his purple bed
And walked upon the house-top with a kingly tread.

Into the markets of the town
Into the streets and gateways he looked down
Serene and comely as the evening star,
And there beheld beside a garden path
A woman bending at her bath.

The King gazed, gazed as the sun
On a distant flower, imparting fire.
He touched his messenger and said,
"Bring this woman to my bedstead."
The servant turned and raised his head:
"Lord, shall I to your chamber bring
The wife of the King's man, Uriah,
The wife of a soldier of the King?"

David leaned on the heavy parapet
And spoke not another word.
Ruddy and beautiful is the Lord's man
And a prince's silence can be heard.

2

With wanton eyes Bath-Sheba
That was faithful in her constancy
Lies on the couch of Judah
And luxuriates in adultery.
With nose-rings and silken veils,
Headbands and earrings and tiaras,
With jewellery on their thighs,
Linen and crisping pins,
Tinkle of gold and silver,
Bath-Sheba laughs and sins.
Her girdle too is spicy,
The kiss between her breasts
Henna-flower and hyacinth.
Honey is her nether lip.

He with his cunning harp
And golden hands that slew the bear
Applies his love and beauty,
Binds and unbinds her hair.
The kiss of David savors
Sweetly of myrrh and holiness;
Before their God the lovers
Dress and undress and dress.

The Ark and the Law are embattled
But War and Time are both beguiled;
She sends to say in a letter,
"My Lord, I am with child."

3

At length Uriah by King David brought
To the royal chair, stands and looks pale
And speaks as one from battle, angry and hot,
Newly released; his thumbs upon his belt
And fingering the proud and studded hilt.
Impatiently he turns and speaks in brief
Of archers fallen, chariots overturned,
Ram-battered towers, and much of running blood,
Friends struck and armor ignominiously
Melted in fire, claimed and fought upon.
To whom the King, quiet and slow of speech,
"Go to thy house and wife; great is your tale,
Great is your journey and your works of blood;
Rest before fighting. Go into thy house."
And now the soldier, white with rage, "O King,
Still in thy tents, the Ark and Israel,
Judah and all abide, and on thy fields
All sway the doubtful outcome of thy God.
For yet the servents of the Almighty stand
Under His captaincy and thine to rule:
Shall I then go into my house and drink,
Lie with my wife and kiss and sleep at noon
But to be taken like a girl alive
Screaming for life and virtue? Now, by my soul
I swear to join my fellows to their last
And fall upon no couches in my death!"

4

King David sealed a letter
And sent it by Uriah's hand
To the chieftain of his armies
That fought to save the Promised Land.

The chieftain read in the letter
That Uriah should wield his sword
In the thick of the hottest battle,
Where he should die for his Lord.

The chieftain wrote to King David
Who lay with Bath-Sheba in a purple bed,
"Abimilech is slain by a woman
And thy servant Uriah also is dead."
King David wrote to his chieftain,
"We fight at the word of Abraham's Lord;
Be courageous and turn the battle
For many and many shall fall by your sword."

But the woman heavily mourned
And wept for Uriah dead.
Not even for the kisses and the words of David
Would she arise and be comforted,
Until King David asked her to wed
And come as a bride to his purple bed,—
And the mourning and the marriage were scarcely done
Before Bath-Sheba bore the King a son.

5

But Jehovah turned upon his servant David
And struck his child so that it lay
Daily and nightly between life and death,
And David rent his clothes and came to pray.

David lay down on the cold earth.

David ate no food and spoke no word.

David lay for seven days and scarcely stirred.

And on the seventh day the servants came and said,

"Lord David, Lord David, the child is dead."
And they feared his grief.

But the King turned from his tears and rose
And washed and anointed his head
And put on spices and majestic clothes
And worshipped the Lord and ate his bread,
And all the people marvelled, but King David said,

"While the child still breathed
I wept and fasted,
For the weight of prayer
Is as gold and fair
In the sight of the Lord;
And my grief has lasted
For seven days
And now the scales are made to yield
And doubt is dead and grief is healed,
I give the Lord praise.
Lay the child upon the sod;
I have felt the hand of God."

And the Lord blessed David with another son,
The greatest of the monarchs, King Solomon.
He wore purple linen; he wore golden shoes;
He was King of the poets, and he ruled the Jews;
He was honored by the nations, the dead and alive;
His songs were a thousand and a thousand and five;
He had a thousand women in a single room;
He built a palace a temple and a golden tomb.
Bath-Sheba was his mother, beautiful to see,
And she lay with King David in adultery.

from
Selected
Poems [1968]

The Bathers

Man and woman, they enter the sea,
The animal-blue, the bovine slippery wave
That, rising, bares its corrugations
And, falling, takes them in its silky teeth
Tightly, while the vast body mills around
Their already watery bodies, till, half blind,
They pass invisibly through its bony sheath,
Swallowed alive and gasping and let go.

They do not even hear the crash of it
Behind them, where it wrecks itself on land,
But are already willed by water,
Weightless and far gone in forgetfulness.

And they are born in that unrisen sky
Out there where all is bright and water-galled
And the loose guts of water tangle them
And then dissolve; where only the dead wave
Comes back awhile, dissipated
And scattered on the wide wash of the sea.

The bathers, blissful in primeval tears,
Forgotten even by the sea itself
That rocks them absently, two bobbing heads,
Onions or oranges
Dumped by the freight of summer on the sea.

They lose even the power of speech;
They must go back to learn;
They make the difficult return
Where nets of water hold them, feel their legs,
Cast ropes of coldness round their bellies,
Trip them, throw gravel at their ankles,
Until, unpredictably, the entire sea
Makes them a path and gives them a push to the beach.

And they lie down between the yellow boats
Where the sun comes and picks them out
And rubs its fire into their sea-pale flesh,
Rubbing their blood, licking their heavy hair,
Breathing upon their words with drying fire.

New Museum

Entering the new museum we feel first
The rubbery values of a doctor's walls,
Cinnamon, buff, gunmetal, rose of gray,
But these almost immediately fade away,
Leaving the windowless white light
That settles only on the works of art—
A far cry from the stained cathedrals where
Masterpieces crack in the bad air
Of candle grease, conversation, and prayer,
Ours is the perfect viewing atmosphere.

Walking around, we are much quieter here
Than in the great basilicas,
The great basilicas of Christendom.
Those freezing niches were the masters' home;
Our galleries warm us like a hotel room
Of cinnamon, powder blue, eggshell of rose,
And yet our painters paint as from a bruise,
The blues neither transparent nor opaque,
The blacks so dry they seem a dust of black.
These are the patterns which our feelings make.

They paint their images as if through smoke,
With now and then a falling coal of red
And now and then a yellow burst, like shock;
They paint the damaged tissue magnified,
The lower land, the structure of the thing;
They paint the darkened luminous optic lake
Through which our eyes, though blind,
See all the lines of force and points of stress
In the scientific field of dark.
These are the patterns which our feelings make.

There is such light in darkness that we see
Blueprints of dreams, child's play, prehistory,
And caves and Altamiras of the mind;
These painters kiss with open eyes to make
Miles of Picassos and the double nose.
Soothed by the blues and blacks, our eyes unclose
To drink great gulps of darkness in;
O skies that fall away time after time
Where tracers of emotion miss the mark
But leave the patterns which our feelings make!

These images have all come home like crows
That cross the hot wheat of the last van Goghs
And cross everything out;
His sorrow saw the thick-skinned peeling sun
Explode above the terrified sunflowers.
Our painters stumble through his private night,
Follow the weak shout of the electric light
Deeper into the caves and offices
Where doctors hang abstractions, blue and black.
These are the patterns which our feelings make.

Manhole Covers

The beauty of manhole covers—what of that?
Like medals struck by a great savage khan,
Like Mayan calendar stones, unliftable, indecipherable,
Not like the old electrum, chased and scored,
Mottoed and sculptured to a turn,
But notched and whelked and pocked and smashed
With the great company names
(Gentle Bethlehem, smiling United States).
This rustproof artifact of my street,
Long after roads are melted away will lie
Sidewise in the grave of the iron-old world,
Bitten at the edges,
Strong with its cryptic American,
Its dated beauty.

Cadillac

Your luna moths bring poems to my eyes,
Your oriflamme brings banners to my slums;
You are fat and beautiful, rich and ugly,
A boiler with gold leaf floral decorations;
You are a hard plush chair with sloping shoulders
In which Victoria, like a kangaroo,
Raises her blazing arms to a poem by Mr. Tennyson.

In the sewing machine of your mind you mend my flags,
Under your forehead fatted sheep are feeding,
Falcons are climbing at unwritten speeds,
Adding machines are singing your arias,
Your motor playing chess with continents,
With Quincy, Illinois, with Hell, New Jersey,
Halting on Oriental rugs in Fez.
Beautiful are your fine cartouches,
Your organ pipes externalized like tusks.

If only I could put my arm around you,
If only I could look you in the eye,
I would tell you a grave joke about turtles' eggs,
But there are always your ostrich plumes,
The hydrangeas drooping between your breasts.
I am afraid of your prosthetic wrists,
The mason jars of your white corpuscles.

For Christmas I will send you Maeterlinck's *Life of the Bee.*

Priests are praying for your beautiful passengers;
Sacraments are burning in your barley-sugar lighthouses;
You carry wild lawyers over yellow bridges;
Your soul as slow as honey coils in vats.

Voluptuous feather-plated Pegasus,
You carry the horizontal thoughtful dead
To golf greens and to sculpture yards of peace.
On leafy springs, O Love, O Death,
Your footfall is the silence that perfects.

I see you everywhere except in dreams.

Western Town

Strange western town at the round edge of night,
Into your sleep the broad-shouldered train
Gentles its way, absorbed in its thunderous quiet,
Shearing off porches of carpenter's gothic,
Gathering bulbs and crocuses of electricity.
Now the green blinds of country stores go down
And arches of gold lettering gleam
Like old asbestos in dead movie houses.

Heart-heavy in the cool compartments
The traveling men turn over in their sleep
As the pale squares of light, newspaper thin,
Fall on their eyelids again and again and again,
Plunging the sleepers into a deeper sleep,
A deeper drift of linen than their dream.

Perhaps a single figure is let down
In the hometown dark, or maybe not;
Perhaps only the sleepy sacks of mail
Or a lone coffin come by rail
At rest now on a sketchy cart. Tomorrow,
Somewhere the city will take the train apart.

Party in Winter

Through jaggedy cliffs of snow, along sidewalks of glass,
Footing unsure, as on a fun-house floor,
A little girl goes, all dressed in black, a Prince
Hamlet himself. In black velvet dress
(under her coat), black stockings (really tights)
And patent leather pumps, solemn white face,
And finally white frill blouse and a gold locket
As a finishing touch, she makes her way,
Bearing an enormous pink and tinfoil box
Tied with a bow of deeper pink.

The box reflects its blush along the high snow walls
As the little prince slips hurriedly up the path
And turns three doors away like a live toy
Into the castle of the birthday party.

Calling the Child

From the third floor I beckon to the child
Flying over the grass. As if by chance
My signal catches her and stops her dance
Under the lilac tree;
And I have flung my net at something wild
And brought it down in all its loveliness.
She lifts her eyes to mine reluctantly,
Measuring in my look our twin distress.

Then from the garden she considers me
And, gathering joy, breaks from the closing net
And races off like one who would forget
That there are nets and snares.
But she returns and stands beneath the tree
With great solemnity, with legs apart,
And wags her head at last and makes a start
And starts her humorous marching up the stairs.

A Garden in Chicago

In the mid-city, under an oiled sky,
I lay in a garden of such dusky green
It seemed the dregs of the imagination.
Hedged round by elegant spears of iron fence
My face became a moon to absent suns.
A low heat beat upon my reading face;
There rose no roses in that gritty place
But blue-gray lilacs hung their tassels out.
Hard zinnias and ugly marigolds
And one sweet statue of a child stood by.

A gutter of poetry flowed outside the yard,
Making me think I was a bird of prose;
For overhead, bagged in a golden cloud,
There hung the fatted souls of animals,
While at my eyes bright dots of butterflies
Turned off and on like distant neon signs.

Assuming that this garden still exists,
One ancient lady patrols the zinnias
(She looks like George Washington crossing the Delaware),
The janitor wanders to the iron rail,
The traffic mounts bombastically out there,
And across the street in a pitch-black bar
With midnight mirrors, the professional
Takes her first whiskey of the afternoon—

Ah! It is like a breath of country air.

Lines for a Unitarian Church

Little church of simple steel I-beams
Set among the squat midwestern houses,
You seem to say and I believe
Body and soul are one,
Man for the world and the world only,
For there is no evil.

Little church without a steeple,
Without the cross, the sword-hilt in the sky,
Without the crazed-glass staining the mystic floor,
You seem to say and I believe
Evil does not exist.

Church of laughter, church of light,
No more the gothic hell, psychotic tower,
Barb-wire star, cruel crescent, mandala,
No more the brothel of the nave, chancre of Guilt
In God's love-nest.

Instead, upon your lawn at church o'clock
A native head sunk in the earth,
A native head chin-deep in the land;
Here the eternal native welcomes you
Welcomes your earliest and best nature,
Welcomes the resurrection into touch.

Little church of friendly steel,
No higher than a human house, as strong,
Beautiful in humid Cincinnati,
Beautiful in the world, inside and out.

The House

We walked over here when it was summer field
And every tree for acres had been felled.
A tumbleweed, the roundness of the world,
Steered close to us and ferried up the hill.
We walked to the dark sill of the excavation
And crossed elastic planks above the pit;
There was impressionable paving, open pipe.
We passed within the cage of wooden ribs,
Gleaming with nails all pointing straight at us.
We ducked through vines of poison-colored wires,
Past the bathtub like a sarcophagus
Crated. Masons were clinking spotless bricks
Pragmatically. We opened the first door,
As a man opens a safe deposit box.
We walked on sod covering the earthen wound;
Squares of live rug gave underfoot like flesh.
Keys were mated with reluctant locks.
Current set up its brilliant nervous system.
We walked on wisps of blond excelsior
And read crimped headlines out of packing cases.
We caught three mice in the acoustical tile;
Three little backs were broken on quick springs.
We sawed and tacked and swept and kissed and cursed
And laid in books and wood and bought a set
Of aluminum numbers and shaved the gray new glass
With razor blades. We slept in whited smells,
Undressed uncurtained in a treeless world.

The Poetry Reading

He takes the lectern in his hands
And, like a pilot at his instruments,
Checks the position of his books, the time,
The glass of water, and the slant of light;
Then, leaning forward on guy-wire nerves,
He elevates the angle of his nose
And powers his soul into the evening.

Now, if ever, he must begin to climb
To that established height
Where one hypnotically remains aloft,
But at the thought, as if an engine coughed,
He drops, barely clearing the first three rows,
Then quakes, recovers, and upward swerves,
And hangs there on his perilous turning fans.

O for more altitude, to spin a cloud
Of crystals, as the cloud writes poetry
In nature's wintry sport!
Or for that hundred-engined voice of wings
That, rising with a turtle in its claws,
Speeds to a rock and drops it heavily,
Where it bursts open with a loud report!

Or for that parchment voice of wrinkled vowels,
That voice of all the ages, polyglot,
Sailing death's boat
Past fallen towers of foreign tours—
The shrouded voice troubled with stony texts,
Voice of all souls and of sacred owls,
Darkly intoning from the tailored coat!

Or for the voice of order, witty and good,
Civilizing the ears of the young and rude,
Weaving the music of ideas and forms,
Writing encyclopedias of hope.
Or for that ever higher voice that swarms
Like a bright monkey up religion's rope
To all those vacant thrones.

But he who reads thinks as he drones his song:
What do they think, those furrows of faces,
Of a poet of the middle classes?
Is he a poet at all? His face is fat.

Can the anthologies have his birthday wrong?
He looks more like an aging bureaucrat
Or a haberdasher than a poet of eminence.

He looks more like a Poet-in-Residence

O to be *declassé,* or low, or high,
Criminal, bastard, or aristocrat—
Anything but the norm, the in-between!
Oh, martyr him for his particular vice,
Make him conspicuous at any price,
Save him, O God, from being nice.

Whom the gods love die young. Too late for that,
Too late also to find a different job,
He is condemned to fly from room to room
And, like a parakeet, be beautiful,
Or, like a grasshopper in a grammar school,
Leap for the window that he'll never find,
And take off with a throb and come down blind.

Photographs of the Poets

As if the inner voice had said, *Don't smile,*
Not one is smiling, as photographers prefer,
But each poet has his chin up, so to speak,
And each poet is in profile, as it were.
The compositions on the whole are weak
And yet suggest the formal Brady style.

Poets are good-looking. It's hard to say just why.
The mouths are poor, often the lips are fat,
The hair of an obvious or a dated cut.
It's difficult to point to this or that
Feature—the ears, for instance—and say what
Precisely makes the pictures catch the eye.

In little ovals and cropped squares they pose,
The sensual, the ethereal, and the vain,
And jut their graceful jawbones into view.
Sometimes the cheeks show deeper grooves of pain
Than in most faces. Nevertheless it's true
The really telltale organ is the nose.

The poet's nose is like a bird in flight;
The winged nostrils buff the shining wind.
The poet's nose is like a speeding prow
That splits the silk of waves and leaves behind
The widening incision of the bow;
The poet's nose is like a bull-tongue plow.

But lesser men have noble noses, too.
It is the look that makes the poet's face;
The look of inside-out, the look of wax,
Of wizened innocence and the skinless gaze;
It is the staring mask that never cracks
Or, when it does, splits dangerously through.

Aged and beardless boys with doubled fists
And girls, old girls, in sibylline disguise,
What is it that the popping camera asks
The flickering silence of your rows of eyes?
What light can penetrate your ancient masks
Or the bright glow of your myopic mists?

Tornado Warning

It is a beauteous morning but the air turns sick,
The April freshness seems to rot, a curious smell.
Above the wool-pack clouds a rumor stains the sky,
A fallow color deadening atmosphere and mind.
The air gasps horribly for breath, sucking itself
In spasms of sharp pain, light drifts away.
Women walk on grass, a few husbands come home,
Bushes and trees stop dead, children gesticulate,
Radios warn to open windows, tell where to hide.

The pocky cloud mammato-cumulus comes on,
Downward-projecting bosses of brown cloud grow
Lumps on lymphatic sky, blains, tumors, and dugs,
Heavy cloud-boils that writhe in general disease of sky,
While bits of hail clip at the crocuses and clunk
At cars and windowglass.

                    We cannot see the mouth,
We cannot see the mammoth's neck hanging from cloud,
Snout open, lumbering down ancient Nebraska
Where dinosaur lay down in deeps of clay and died,
And towering elephant fell and billion buffalo.
We cannot see the horror-movie of the funnel-cloud
Snuffing up cows, crazing the cringing villages,
Exploding homes and barns, bursting the level lakes.

Bad Taste, Inc.

I

There is a shop in Paris called Bad Taste
(Le Mauvais Goût) where objets d'art,
Chiefly Victorian, are sold
To wedding couples from the States,
Interior decorators, movie stars,
Rich poets and other sophisticates.
The past peddles the past
To the latest barbarians. Nothing goes to waste:
Yesterday's newspaper, bits of string,
Forgotten comforts, masterpieces.
In Paris nothing goes to waste,
Especially Taste, especially Bad Taste.

II

In America everything goes to waste.
We waste ourselves in the hygienic sun,
We waste the future, burn it to the ground.
Waste in the States is the national industry,
All are consumers—*consume, consume!*
On to the waste pipe, the cloaca americana!

Human Nature

For months and years in a forgotten war
I rode the battle-gray Diesel-stinking ships
Among the brilliantly advertised Pacific Islands,
Coasting the sinister New Guinea Coasts,
All during the killing and hating of a forgotten war.
Now when I drive behind a Diesel-stinking bus
On the way to the university to teach
Stevens and Pound and Mallarmé,
I am homesick for war.

A Drawerful of Eyeglasses

I have a drawerful of eyeglasses
Which Spinoza or Galileo would have given their eyeteeth for:
Green-black prescription glasses,
Glasses for reading or driving,
Even a reading lens for proofreading poems.
What if a tornado ground them up with brick?
What if they were melted by the master-bomb
As the sands of the desert were melted to balls of glass?
What if I couldn't read the latest book
On metaphor or guilt?
What if I had to make up poems in my head
Like Milton or Homer?

Man on Wheels

Cars are wicked, poets think.
Wrong as usual. Cars are part of man.
Cars are biological.
A man without a car is like a clam without a shell.
Granted, machinery is hell,
But carless man is careless and defenseless.
Ford is skin of present animal.
Automobile is shell.
You get yourself a shell or else.

You Call These Poems?

In Hyderabad, city of blinding marble palaces,
White marble university,
A plaything of the Nizam, I read some poetry
By William Carlos Williams, American.
And the educated and the suave Hindus
And the well-dressed Moslems said,
"You call those things poems?
Are those things poems?"

For years I used to write poems myself
That pleased the Moslems and Hindus of culture,
Telling poems in iambic pentameter,
With a masculine inversion in the second foot,
Frozen poems with an ice-pick at the core,
And lots of allusions from other people's books.

Emily Dickinson and Katherine Anne Porter

I

Emily Dickinson's father yanked on the Baptist bell
To call the townspeople to see the sunset,
And the Baptists saw the glory of the sunset
And went home to stained-glass darkness, awfully disappointed
That something really hideous hadn't happened,
Like Hell or the atom bomb.
Old man Dickinson who also fed the sparrows over the snow
With grain from his barn (age seventy-one)
And hid until he saw them peck it up.

"And drove the fastest horse in town."

II

And when Dylan Thomas was introduced
To Katherine Anne Porter in a room full of people,
He stooped and picked her up below the thighs
And raised her to the ceiling like a drink,
And held her straight in the slack-jawed smoke-blue air
Two minutes, five minutes, seven minutes,
While everybody wondered what it meant
To toast the lady with her own body
Or hold her to the light like a plucked flower.

257

A Modest Funeral

Death passed by on fervid rubber wheels.
Three broad mortuary Cadillacs,
Flying modest pennants low on the fenders,
Led the procession, followed by a covey
Of medium-priced cars, with no overcrowding,
And some with just a driver at the wheel,
But the whole cluster with headlights lit,
As is the law and custom of the thoroughfare.

Only at the rear was there any sign of jostling,
Any suggestion of impatient thought
At foolish delay, or *Where's the funeral!*

Death passed at moderate speed and slowed the counter-traffic
To a respectful twenty, making it almost veer,
As when one hears a siren in the distance.

Then it was gone, the funeral with its flags
And fine sparkling lights, like tears in the eyes,
Gone to the silvered fences at the edge of town,
And the soft gravel of the cemetery.

Connecticut Valley

Call it the richest pocket of the world,
Which rumored in the ear of Milton's breed
Once bore the freeborn Englishman across,
Or from God-ridden Massachusetts, down.

A while the Indian stinking from his paint
Stalked the white villages and counted scalps
But turned, lacking concealment, to the hills,
Or else fell, richer by a musket ball,

Leaving the land divided, as were fit,
Between the men with implements to scratch,
Rescratch and smooth and currycomb the dirt
March after March unto the present hour.

Good Yankees these, and round about the sane
Practical hearts who fashioned all the nails
For the new nation, carving in spare time
Wooden nutmegs to sell to willing fools;

Ruling themselves by blue laws, painting pure
The plain church, blending beauty with the snow.
Death for adultery in the pretty towns
And strictness in the fields for centuries.

After three hundred years the motorist
Happening by may marvel at these streets
Where every dwelling bears the building date
In homage to the beauty of great age;

Where every ghost is laid, knowing how well
The pride of house is kept, both in the fields
Where dark tobacco sweetens under gauze,
Cows calve, corn stretches to the yellow sun;

And where on lawns the Sunday gentry meet,
Insurance writers, toolmakers in tweeds,
The fibrous sons and daughters of the state
Driving hard bargains through the afternoon.

In India

In India, the people form among the trees
With a rubbery quiet; on farthest roads
Surround you with a rubbery tread.
I stand in their circles of wonder like a light
Shining in eyes grown vague with centuries
Of stunned obedience and heartbreaking loads,
Not tall, I tower above them by a head;
Pale, I pass through their never-ending night.

A crow came to my window by the sea
At four o'clock in the Taj Mahal Hotel;
He cocked his eye and when I turned my back
Flew to my tea tray with a hideous clack
Of beak and claws, turning over the tea
And making off with the cake. The crow did well,
For down below me, where the street was black
With white-clad Hindus, what was there to take?

And foreigners say the poverty is the cause,
Thinking that gold can cure the old disease,
Thinking that oil can make the old wheel turn.
I see a new landmark on the long skyline,
An edifice of seamless stone and glass
Topped by the great word *Standard* in the skies.
Toward the Arabian Sea I watch it burn
And, being American, feel that it is mine!

And still the native voices, soft as sand,
Cry, "Master! Master!" as a professional saint
Might roll his eyes and faint into his god
In the middle of traffic. Still they call aloud
"Sahib, Master!" and hold out their hand.
And lovely women with a moon of paint
Daubed on their foreheads shake hands and fade
Into silence, bowing with a praying bow.

These beautiful, small millions turn to stone
Before your eyes, become soft sculpture swarming up
The slant of temples, where their thighs protrude
Half out of joint, the angles of their arms
Twist in voluptuous torsion, and their bones
Fold into symbols pliable as rope.
The walls are sluggish with their multitude
Of gods and dancers and half-human forms.

But are they gods or droppings of the gods?
Is this the mire in which they all submerge,
This bog of holiness which ingurgitates
Prophet and hero, turning them to stone?
Which are the deities, which the human clods?
Or in this jungle do they truly merge?
And where is Reason in this hive of faith—
The one god missing from this pantheon?

I see a new god carved in fresh relief,
The brown saint in the shining spectacles
Who took the hand of the untouchables,
Who wove all India from a skein of thread.
Now he and all their spinning wheels are gone,
For a young Hindu, under whose homespun
Lay a revolver, knelt and, in good faith,
Received his blessing and then shot him dead.

California Winter

It is winter in California, and outside
Is like the interior of a florist shop:
A chilled and moisture-laden crop
Of pink camellias lines the path; and what
Rare roses for a banquet or a bride,
So multitudinous that they seem a glut!

A line of snails crosses the golf-green lawn
From the rosebushes to the ivy bed;
An arsenic compound is distributed
For them. The gardener will rake up the shells
And leave in a corner of the patio
The little mound of empty snails, like skulls.

By noon the fog is burnt off by the sun
And the world's immensest sky opens a page
For the exercises of a future age;
Now jet planes draw straight lines, parabolas,
And x's, which the wind, before they're done,
Erases leisurely or pulls to fuzz.

It is winter in the valley of the vine.
The vineyards crucified on stakes suggest
War cemeteries, but the fruit is pressed,
The redwood vats are brimming in the shed,
And on the sidings stand tank cars of wine,
For which bright juice a billion grapes have bled.

And skiers from the snow line driving home
Descend through almond orchards, olive farms,
Fig tree and palm tree—everything that warms
The imagination of the wintertime.
If the walls were older one would think of Rome:
If the land were stonier one would think of Spain.

But this land grows the oldest living things,
Trees that were young when Pharaohs ruled the world,
Trees whose new leaves are only just unfurled.
Beautiful they are not; they oppress the heart
With gigantism and with immortal wings;
And yet one feels the sumptuousness of this dirt.

It is raining in California, a straight rain
Cleaning the heavy oranges on the bough,
Filling the gardens till the gardens flow,
Shining the olives, tiling the gleaming tile,
Waxing the dark camellia leaves more green,
Flooding the daylong valleys like the Nile.

from
White-
Haired
Lover

There Was That Roman Poet

There was that Roman poet who fell in love at fifty-odd.
My God, *Venus,* goddess of love, he cried,
Venus, for Christsake, for the love of God,
Don't do that to me!
Don't let me fall in love, a man of my age.
I beg you on my knobby knees, lay off.
Basta! I've had enough—not only that,
NON SUM QUALIS ERAM, Jesus Christ!
How do you know I can get it up!

The laughter of the goddess cool as hell
Pinged like a Cellini shell.
Priceless, she said, showing her teeth, clacking her castanets, stomping her
    feet.
And what has age to do with that, Quintus, she said,
And put that in your Classical Dictionary . . .
And went her way in a wild odor of roses and garlic.

You Lay Above Me

You lay above me on that beautiful day,
Your dark eyes made more dark with tiny wings
You drew to prick my kisses with beestings.
Your russet hair in heavy brushstrokes lay
Against the pastel of the Nebraska sky
And all around the stippled poplar trees
Framed you like an unpainted masterpiece.
Some birds spoke out and airplanes coming over,
And now and then a farmer peered our way
Where we were stretched out on the new green grass
On a green blanket, to see a white-haired lover
And a wine-colored, flower-printed creature,
As mythologically dark and dazzling as
The sun that forces frozen earth to nature.

I Am the Clown

I am the clown that laughs and cries into your life
Knocking you down and picking you up,
And you are the last woman in the laughing arena of my life.
In the darkened garden of upturned faces
I fall in terror from the absurd highwire
Into the love-net of your spangled arms,
And when you wipe the greasepaint of my tears
And when you rearrange my smile
With tears and laughter in the front seat of a car
Aimlessly floating through obscure back streets and over the humpback
    country roads
Which send up dust clouds of applause into the rawsilk scarves of sky,
We kiss to the patriotic ridiculous roll of drums
And fall into the spaceless spaces of each other.

How Do You Walk?

How do you walk? You walk into my arms,
Into my kiss, into the eye of my life's storm.
You walk (all similes are silly in my love for you)
You walk as if you were carrying the Taj Mahal.
Your neck is like a Watusi woman towering above the grasses of your
    tigerish clothes,
Your tribal shoulders where my fingers close and feed and my lips graze
    like sheep-crazed shepherds.
You walk in anger and in glorious pride as if you had lost a brilliant
    naval battle,
Your cut smile belies your perspicuous eyes,
Your earrings tremble and your breasts rise like waves of liquid in your
    coming toward me.
Your hips powerful and civilized make idiots of willow trees plying the
    prairie winds,
You carry your hard-soft hands as if they were not yours but mine.
Is it your long proud legs that carry you into my vision like rhyme?
You walk as if you were carrying a love-child,
You walk as if you were marrying me,
And your sensitive head turns slightly side to side
As not to see the lovely commotion of your passing,
Where you have come from but only where you are going.
Where are you going? You are going into your beauty
And it is I who am opening all the doors as you pass
From room to room of your life till you walk to my grave.

Aubade

Et c'est la fin pour quoy sommes ensemble.

What dawn is it?

The morning star stands at the end of your street as you watch me turn to laugh a kind of goodbye, with love-crazed head like a white satyr moving through wet bushes.

The morning star bursts in my eye like a hemorrhage as I enter my car in a dream surrounded by your heavenly-earthly smell.

The steering wheel is sticky with dew,

The golf course is empty, husbands stir in their sleep desiring, and though no cocks crow in suburbia, the birds are making a hell of a racket.

Into the newspaper dawn as sweet as your arms that hold the old new world, dawn of green lights that smear the empty streets with come and go.

It is always dawn when I say goodnight to you,

Dawn of wrecked hair and devastated beds,

Dawn when protective blackness turns to blue and lovers drive sunward with peripheral vision.

—To improvise a little on Villon,

Dawn is the end for which we are together.

My house of loaded ashtrays and unwashed glasses, tulip petals and columbine that spill on the table and splash on the floor,

My house full of your dawns,

My house where your absence is presence,

My slum that loves you, my bedroom of dustmice and cobwebs, of local paintings and eclectic posters, my bedroom of rust neckties and divorced mattresses, and of two of your postcards, *Pierrot with Flowers* and *Young Girl with Cat,*

My bed where you have thrown your body down like a king's ransom or a boa constrictor.

But I forgot to say: May passed away last night,

May died in her sleep.

That May that blessed and kept our love in fields and motels.

I erect a priapic statue to that May for lovers to kiss as long as I'm in print, and polish as smooth as the Pope's toe.

This morning came June of spirea and platitudes,

This morning came June discreetly dressed in gray,

June of terrific promises and lawsuits.

And where are the poems that got lost in the shuffle of spring?

Where is the poem about the eleventh of March, when we raised the battleflag of dawn?

Where is the poem about the coral necklace that whipped your naked breasts in leaps of love?

The poem concerning the ancient lover we followed through your beautiful sleeping head?

The fire-fountain of your earthquake thighs and your electric mouth?
Where is the poem about the little one who says my name and watches us
    almost kissing in the sun?
The vellum stretchmarks on your learned belly,
Your rosy-fingered nightgown of nylon and popcorn,
Your razor that caresses your calves like my hands?
Where are the poems that are already obsolete, leaves of last month, a very
    historical month?
Maybe I'll write them, maybe I won't, no matter,
And this is the end for which we are together.
Et c'est la fin pour quoy sommes ensemble.

Words for a Wall-Painting

On this wall like child I write I love you
Public and private graffiti of my heart,
Sun of your love lays bare these simple lines
Like a Pompeiian bedroom lit with gold
And black Vesuvian plume. As pink as stone
Your hand uncovers me. Round as a bay
Your form encircles my form night and day,
And deep as Mare Nostrum with sweet salt
Washes whole centuries of sleep away.
This is the time of finding hour by hour
The streets and alleys of our ecstasy.
This is the place to sign my syllables
Of deep relief on tiny tiles of sound,
And may my words still stand when the wall falls.
This is a poem to write upon your wall,
My wall, our wall, to meet us in the eye
In the dawnlight of Chicago furry-gray
When garbage truck groans in the alley-way,
Sparrows chitter and pigeons make their moan.
On this wall like child I write I love you
I write I love you in our private moan.
I paint I love you Teri and sign Karl.

New, and Uncollected Poems

A Prayer for Rain

Meteorological god, though hidden behind a cloud
   of technological atheism, this thirsty valley
needs you. As far north as Shasta levels have fallen,
   exposing the red-ribbed naked banks. Will you now,
after the world-renown of this super-valley
   hit the rich rancher and the poor chicano equally?
I in my own suburb bespangled with pomegranate and lemon
   have reset the sprinklers voluntarily, without
however, putting a brick in the toilet tank.
   The High Sierras are bare and the rice paddies
are mud-cracked, dust devils are doing their dervish,
   lawns are in shock, swimming pools filling with dirt.
Forget, father of waters, these waste land tactics;
   let in the lows from Alaska, or curving up
from the south, first gently wetten the dust, then gradually
   open your million invisible spigots for a steady
weeklong downpour, just as in winter you have always done.
   Pisser on high, keep your mythological promise
of this as yet unpaved-over prelapsarian Eden.

Sea Ranch

Not on that geologic strand haunted by eco-freaks,
      where houses are all owned by orthodontists
and humanities professors, cars are buried in classy crypts
      and the architecture is super-Superior Cal-
ifornia, practically invisible, expertly weathered
      to fit the cloth of the silvery marshes and meadows
and suede foothills; not on that rock-girt shore with abrupt
      headlands, inspiration of thousands of amateur
oils for sale in minor restaurants, do I cast my longing,
      but rather here in this valley flat as North Platt
or den Haag, the coastal range outside the garden,
      and on a rare clear day the High Sierras
walling us off from the national weather. This is as far
      as I go, cannot within my inner eye
gaze on the gluttony of the fat Pacific, but follow
      its seagulls inward blown when the wind is right.

T.S.E.

Coming slowly down the aisle,
Mounting the podium with baronial tread,
Very solemn and slightly stooped,
As if in awe of his stupendous stature,
The responsibility which he has created,
The hush he has summoned,
He carries his poems in two slim volumes,
Holding them lightly in one hand
And touched by the fingers of the other hand,
Sensing rather than carrying his books,
His mythic poetry that has stunned the world.

W.B.Y.

Shooting me in my study a cameraman
Panned upward to my highest shelf of books,
The X-Y-Z's that end the alphabet
Of poets of every flag, when suddenly
He spied a perfect spiderweb,
Invisible except to the professional eye.
There from the ceiling delicately hung
The draglines and the swathing bands
Of viscid spider-silk caging and veiling
What journalists would call one of the greats,
The Collected Works of William Butler Yeats.

W.H.A.

Without him many of us would have never happened
But would have gone on being Georgians or worse;
We all recall how he galloped into verse
On Skelton's nag and easily reopened

Eighteenth-century prosody like a can of worms,
And there like Alice on a checkerboard
Careened through Marx and Freud and Kierkegaard
Dazzled and dazzling all the ideas and forms,

And camped out in the United States to wrinkle
Like an Indian squaw to await the Nobel Prize
And study savages with paleface eyes
And sit on Oxford Dictionaries and rankle.

God bless this poet who took the honest chances;
God bless the live poets whom his death enhances.

The Accountant

We went to him because we thought
     He was a Jew. His name was Low,
Wasn't it? And we were ushered in-
     To the presence of a tall and courtly
Chinese man, whose office over-
     Looked what seemed the entire West.

Each year we pay our ceremonial
     Visit for the W 2.
This doesn't take much time although
     The visit lasts the accountable hour
In which we discuss our families,
     Education, politics, in that order.
One thinks there should be tea perhaps,
     But no, only the ceremonious
Fifty-minute hour passed
     Pleasantly till we are done,
The accountant rises and we are led
     Back to the blond receptionist
Where we shake hands and smile and say
     Goodbye, good luck, until next year.

The Mezuzah

A hand in morning banged the door,
    not hard but with a kindly fist,
splashing my mercurial dream
    to beads of light. I turned and thought
it has to be a Christian there
    banging at my bright front door,
and turned back to my sleep.
Let him leave his literature, I said,
    and put a pillow on my head.

Once on a secular afternoon
    two Adventists or Mormons came
(who always come in twos like nuns)
    to confront me or affront me.
I took their literature in hand
    and with a kind of smile assayed
to point the error of their way.
    Rather I pointed to the jamb
where I had tacked the doorpost prayer
    hidden in its small bronze case
to consecrate the house. I said
    that is the holy letter Shin,
that is the secret name of God;
    inside are praise and promises.
Sirs, when you see that talisman
    you really ought to skip that house.

They looked at it and glanced at it
    and nodding wisely went their way.

The Old Poet

Coming to the end of his dated poems in the complete edition, knowing what he did not—the date already written, how many weeks were left, the very number of minutes, I read as with a burning-glass. And so many years between the opening page and a man lingering over the final words in a foreign country—after which there is only an index.

That radiance of old poets (those who surrendered power with a smile). In his own city he renames the streets, the ships, the bars. History comes to his hand like a tame pigeon. One of his sentences hangs in the square like the plume of a volcano. Real speech, real life are unwritten. Only these lines have a tendency to remain forever. Cities with poetry remember him. Cities without poetry.

Bellow

Saul when he laughs laughs at you or with you (it's the same thing in his
    case), a delightful factious laugh at your expense. There's anger in it,
    a rabbinical impatience with the dull. (Here there would be such a
    laugh.) Mixing a powerful sense of fidelity with an equally powerful
    sense of the absurd, he evolves Yiddish, language without pedigree.
    Poetry with him is on the up-and-up, only there isn't any. Tough as
    a gangster, tender as a child. Everybody is a character to be. (Here
    there would be such a laugh.) He doesn't piddle away on earnest
    causes. At the core of things lies the ridiculous, ready to louse up the
    language. He wants the best for himself and has got it and it makes
    him groan. He understands that the fame of others is like the best
    resort (no Jews allowed). A master of timing. The good thing about
    it is that it's past rebellion. Style in his eyes (here there would be such
    a laugh, a double one). He'd be hard to be married to, though he
    would supply the works: excitement, cruelty, sensuality, over-pro-
    tectiveness of children, and unmistakable power of self.

And vision—Henderson standing under—"the beautiful propellers."

285

Winery at Napa

It is very quiet in the factory of wine, the Napa Valley outside, rich respectable paradise. Here in the cool it is silent as a library. Wine is sleeping in those Brobdingnagian vats or gurgling through miles of pipe. Oak vats or glistening stainless steel for fermentation. Under the stopcocks puddles of purple; drops find their way into standing buckets. Everywhere the lovely stain in the damp, anesthetic, slightly vinegar air.

In the wine-tasting lobby an art show in progress. Critics and guests exchange the window-views of the vineyards for the paintings, and for each other.

Outside, under the official palms, the tankcars wait to glide along the valley floors with an air of boredom and matter-of-fact.

Sacramento Winos

In Sacramento the winos float across the intersections with soft silky colorless
beards. Or red headbands and blueblack beards. Among these pirates
are real Indians. They stand or squat in knots or clusters, a fashion
show of arrivals and departures. Huge blue policemen, in car or out,
loom up at intervals. But there's no trouble, scarcely any noise. It's ten
o'clock in the morning and the winos are already deep in their dream-
work. They decorate the fountains of the Thirties, forty years late,
smack in front of the City Hall.

Walking, they barely touch the ground, these anchorites, poets of back alleys
and derelict hotels, world travelers, and are very much at home, these
philosophers.

A woman bursts from a door as if escaping. She checks her speed in the
light, lurches a little, then walks at a run three quarters of a block.
Her dress is filthy, her hair is wild, her eyes roll. Whereupon she
maneuvers into a wine-shop.

Tobacconists

Tobacconists mad as poets, more voluble than barbers, brilliant as schizophrenics, you are a brotherhood. Is it your traffic with scholars, your intimacy with the milder narcotics and exotic scraps of wood that makes you a class? You have the assurance of foreign movie actors, the dogmatism of physicians. Those bins and tins and canisters intimidate whole sections of the population. How did you rise above politics and the narrow event? Your sublime orality, your jewelry trays of pipes, anachronistic foamy meerschaums, gold-banded corncobs, all the Victorian bric-a-brac of contentment, can these artifacts survive, O speed, O pot, O snow?

Nō Mask

Washing the face of my Nō, I wash it with brillo, gently, not to scratch
the even lacquer of this fine mask. It is the princess mask, worn by
a man in the plays. The face is an absolute oval, painted dead white,
shaped in defiance of natural beauty. It is rimmed with black to sug-
gest the hair, forehead as high as the conventional Shakespearean
dome, eyebrows set at a ridiculous height, sketched rather than stated.
The nose is broad and bulbous, the eyes pierced at the pupil. Seeing
through these small holes, the actor dances stiffly and with classical
dignity.

Chin large, mouth crimson, but the teeth are black. Blacked out like
cauterized gums—yet they are beautiful! Like the sounds forced from
the wooden lips, sounds on the hair-line of hysteria, the Nō face is
unearthly, speaking with spirits or hanging on my wall. It converses
with the tilt of light, as versatile as flesh.

Pipe-clay, holy color, Commodore Perry closed that show.

Mozart's Jew

Much as I enjoy your minor immortality, Da Ponte, I marvel where you
lie. New Jersey; New York; something like that. My God, Da Ponte,
you gave Mozart the words for all that music. And why do you make
me uneasy? Because you were a Jew, Emanuele Conegliano? Because
you were a Catholic priest, harried from town to town, country to
country, for your love affairs? Because you lie and cover up in your
book, only to be caught red-handed? What difference does it make.
You called yourself a poet, you fraud, but you had guts. Writing
three plays for three different composers at once, and one of them
Mozart. And his the *Don Giovanni!* Writing twelve hours on end, like
a Hollywood hack. And plenty of Tokay on the table (*goût de terroir*)
and lots of Seville tobacco, not to mention the sixteen-year-old girl,
your mistress during this project. I like you Da Ponte. And finally
bounced out of Europe itself, to open a grocery store in New Jersey,
that's almost too much. And failing at it, of course. And yet I think
you must have been the first to say of Mozart: the greatest composer,
past, present and future. That little bit took genius to say. And the
Emperor Joseph liked you. And Casanova, jailed for reading Voltaire.
All of you Don Giovannis I like, and you especially, Mozart's Jew, Da
Ponte.

Evangelist

To hate the handsome evangelist is not enough, his eyes so pale he's eyeless,
a Greek statue. Sneering him down is impossible and he won't reason
away like kings. Jefferson sat on a box in the Charlottesville Square
listening in dismay to such. Besides, he has an element of truth. They
all have an element of truth, witch-doctors, freedom peddlars, oracles
of God. Vulgar to mention his vast estate, luncheons with presidents
and queens, the congregation numbering in the millions. No bible-
thumper, he speaks southernly, softens his way into the stirring
bowels of upturned untold souls. He gives them each their god of
love to carry pregnantly to bed. He wets their hearts with eyelessness.
He waves their blood like napkins. Something of the killer about him,
witch-doctor, freedom peddlar, oracle of God. He points the way to
Love like a popular song, then leaves his millions gasping on the
beach. They writhe and groan and spill dry tears. Their eyes redden
and ready for war.

He smiles to the left, he smiles to the right, and nobody yet has ever heard
him laugh.

from
Adult
Bookstore

A Parliament of Poets

Two hundred poets are sitting side by side
In the government auditorium,
Waiting their turn to mount the stage
And read five minutes' worth of poems,
And then sit down again, still side by side,
The young, the old, the crazy, the sane
In alphabetical order.
Some rant their lines, some plead and some intone,
Some bellow and some simply talk.

Outside along the curb there waits a line
Of blue government buses
To carry the poets to the White House to shake hands
With the young President. The President
Is interested in shaking hands with the poets
And possibly saying something to each.

But when the alphabet has run its course
The chairman takes the lectern to announce
That the trip to the White House is called off,
The visit has been postponed
Or canceled for an indefinite period.

It appears that the President has chosen this hour
To warn the nation that a fleet of freighters,
Carrying atomic warheads on their decks
Visibly, are moving towards the coast of Cuba,
And that the President has ordered our fleet
To intercept and blockade the invaders.

And the parliament of poets disintegrates,
Some going to their hotel rooms to pack,
Some to the dark bars, some to the streets
To gaze up at the vacant Washington sky.

The Humanities Building

All the bad Bauhaus comes to a head
In this gray slab, this domino, this plinth
Standing among the olives or the old oak trees,
As the case may be, and whatever the clime.
No bells, no murals, no gargoyles,
But rearing like a fort with slits of eyes
Suspicious in the aggregate, its tons
Of concrete, glaciers of no known color,
Gaze down upon us. Saint Thomas More,
Behold the Humanities Building!
                              On the top floor
Are one and a half professors of Greek,
Kicked upstairs but with the better view,
And two philosophers, and assorted Slavics;
Then stacks of languages coming down,
Mainly the mother tongue and its dissident children
(History has a building all its own)
To the bottom level with its secretaries,
Advisors, blue-green photographic light
Of many precious copying machines
Which only the girls are allowed to operate.
And all is bathed in the cool fluorescence
From top to bottom, justly distributed
Light, Innovation, Progress, Equity;
Though in my cell I hope and pray
Not to be confronted by
A student with a gun or a nervous breakdown,
Or a girl who closes the door as she comes in.

The Old Guard sits in judgment and wears ties,
Eying the New in proletarian drag,
Where the Assistant with one lowered eyelid
Plots against Tenure, dreaming of getting it;

And in the lobby, under the bulletin boards,
The Baudelairean forest of posters
For Transcendental Meditation, Audubon Group,
"The Hunchback of Notre Dame," Scientology,
Arab Students Co-op, "Case of the Curious Bride,"
Two students munch upon a single sandwich.

Adult Bookstore

Round the green fountain thick with women
Abstract in the concrete, water trickling
Between their breasts, wetting their waists
Girdled with wheat, pooling in the basin,
The walker pauses, shrugs, peregrinates
To the intersection, section of the city
Where forgotten fountains struggle for existence,
Shops have declined to secondhand
And marginal cultures collect like algae.
Dubious enterprises flourish here,
The massage parlor, the adult bookstore.

Their windows are either yellowed or blacked
Or whited or redded out,
Bold lettering proclaiming No Minors Allowed,
Bachelor Books, Adult Films and Cartoons.

The doorway jogs to the right at a strict angle
And everything from the street is invisible,
Keeping the law and clutching the illusion.
Inside, the light is cold and clean and bright,
Everything sanitary, wrapped in cellophane

Which flashes messages from wall to wall
Of certain interest to the eye that reads
Or does not read: Randy, Coit,
Sex Hold-Up, Discipline, Ghetto Male,
Images of cruelty, ideas for the meek,
Scholarly peeks at French, English and Greek,
And everywhere the more than naked nude
Mystery called the wound that never heals.

Or there a surgical cabinet all glass:
Pink plastic phalli, prickly artifact,
Enlarger finger-small or stallion-size,
Inflatable love partner, five feet four.
Lotions, Hot Melt, super-double-dong,
Battery dildo (origin obscure),
Awakeners of the tired heart's desire
When love goes wrong.

The expense of spirit in a waste of shame
Is sold forever to the single stag
Who takes it home in a brown paper bag.

Girls Working in Banks

Girls working in banks wear bouffant hair and shed
In their passage over the rather magnificent floors
Tiny shreds of perforated paper, like body flakes.
They walk through rows of youngish vice-presidents
With faraway looks, who dandle pencils and tend to ignore
The little tigerish lights flashing on their telephones.
When the girls return to their stations behind a friendly grid
They give out money neatly or graciously take it,
For not far from them the great interior glow of a vault
Built out of beaten dimes, stands open, shines,
Beaming security without ostentation.
If you glance inside it, there's nothing to be seen
But burnished drawers and polished steel elbows
Of the great machine of the door. It's a speckless world
With nobody inside it, like the best room in the gallery
Awaiting the picture which is still in a crate.
The girls change places frequently, moving their own addresses
From Open to Closed, Next Counter, or they walk away
With surprising freedom behind a wall or rise up on escalators
Past aging and well-groomed guards whose pistols seem
Almost apologetic as they watch people
Bending over Formica stand-up desks writing
With ballpoint pens attached to rosary chains,
After which the people select a queue in which they stand
Pious, abashed at the papery transactions,
And eventually walk with the subtlest sense of relief
Out of revolving doors into the glorious anonymous streets.

Crossing Lincoln Park

Dit le corbeau, jamais plus.—Mallarmé

Car locked, I started home across the grass,
A kind of island with a stand of oaks
Washed round on all sides by the swish of cars,
To where I lived, a hundred yards in view.
Quarried apartments rose on every hand,
Scoriac Gothic shouldering solid glass
Hemming me in, reflecting a blank sky.
Briefcase and I happily homeward strode
Through ankle-grass, when something at my shoe
Darkly turned over, what I never knew,
For down came the crow and with a sudden blow,
Its great wings beating, slashed at my face
With croak and scream and yellow beak
Screeching me out. I did not stop to think
But leapt and sprinted toward the curb, the bird
Cursing, crisscrossing, driving at my face,
Crashing my shoulders with its filthy wings.
Ugly, omnivorous offal-eating crow,
Bird of ill omen,
Eater of turd and dead fish, get thy beak
From out my heart! My eyeglasses flew off,
I stumbled forward, clutching my briefcase,
Fanning away the bird with naked hand,
Until I reached the street where solid cars
Bumper to bumper blocked my flight,
And still the crow surrounded me and struck
Till I broke through and in the door and up
The elevator to the velvet hall
And to the door and in, where your bright smile
Changed instantly to—"White!" you said.
"Your face whiter than chalk!"

The White Negress

(Brancusi—Chicago Art Institute)

Who has not seen Brancusi's White Negress?
O quarryman who cut her from the mountain,
Did you see her breathing in the mountain?
Geology, what did you have in mind!

Slightly smaller than life, her head
Stands up like a magnolia bud
In snowy marble,
With a little marble ribbon tying her hair in the back,
Matching her slightly spread nose
And her pretty protruding lips,
The White Negress in all her marble beauty,
So black, so white!

Jefferson's Greeting

At the foot of his mountain he stops the carriage
For the first glimpse of the white Palladian dome
That tops his house; then up the bluish hills
Of Albemarle, past garden and vine,
When suddenly there burst from every side
The blacks, who pull the horses from the shafts
And haul him like a chariot up the drive,
Cheering, dancing, crying his return,
Lifting the master bodily
Up the steps and over the threshold,
Kissing his hands and feet, even the ground
He passes over, the great Virginian home,
Whose wilderness he carved into decorum.

My Father's Funeral

Lurching from gloomy limousines we slip
On the warm baby-blanket of Baltimore snow,
Wet flakes smacking our faces like distraught
Kisses on cheeks, and step upon the green
Carpet of artificial grass which crunches
Underfoot, as if it were eating, and come
To the canopy, a half-shelter which provides
A kind of room to enclose us all, and the hole,
And the camp chairs, and following after,
The scrolly walnut coffin
That has my father in it.

Minutes ago in the noncommittal chapel
I saw his face, not looking himself at all
In that compartment hinged to open and shut,
A vaudeville prop with a small waxen man,
"So cold," the widow said and shied away
In a wide arc of centrifugal motion,
To come again to stand like me beside,
In the flowerless room with electric candelabra.
If there is among our people any heaven,
We are rather ambiguous about it
And tend to ignore the subject.

The rabbi's eulogy is succinct,
Accurate and sincere, and the great prayer
That finishes the speech is simply praise
Of God, the god my father took in stride
When he made us learn Hebrew and shorthand,
Taught us to be superior, as befits
A nation of individual priests.
At my sister's house we neither pray nor cry
Nor sit, but stand and drink and joke,
So that one of the youngsters says
It's more like a cocktail party.

For Dylan's dandy villanelle,
For Sylvia's oath of damnation one reserves
A technical respect. To Miller's Willie
And Lewis's Babbitt I demur.
My father was writing a book on salesmanship
While he was dying; it was his book of poems,
Destined to be unpublished. He hadn't time
To master books but kept the house well stocked

With random volumes, like a ship's library,
Rows and rows of forgotten classics,
Books for the sake of having books.

My father in black knee-socks and high shoes
Holding a whip to whip a top upstreet;
My father the court stenographer,
My father in slouch hat in the Rockies,
My father kissing my mother,
My father kissing his secretary,
In the high-school yearbook captioned Yid,
In synagogue at six in the morning praying
Three hundred and sixty-five days for his mother's rest,
My father at my elbow on the bimah
And presiding over the Sabbath.

In the old forgotten purlieus of the city
A Jewish ghetto in its day, there lie
My father's father, mother and the rest,
Now only a ghetto lost to time,
Ungreen, unwhite, unterraced like the new
Cemetery to which my father goes.
Abaddon, the old place of destruction;
Sheol, a new-made garden of the dead
Under the snow. Shalom be to his life,
Shalom be to his death.

The Sense of Beauty

The human form is seldom beautiful,
Less beautiful than animal in zoo.
The human mind with beauty is accursed,
Man being esthetic animal.
Man is the only beast that measures busts,
Bottoms and teeth and feet and length of bone.
Man of all living things worships the new,
Man of all creatures thinks he must be first,
Thinks he must intellectualize his lusts.
Man is the only animal alone,
And only man invents his Caliban.
The only esthetic animal is man.

Therefore a prince in cloth of paradise
Would keep a dwarf to emphasize his state;
A whore therefore, a power behind the throne,
Would lead her monkey on a gold device.
Cripples strike fear in children and in hags.
People stare into mirrors not from pride
But to decide if it is not too late
To reconstruct the esthetic of the bone.
Charles Baudelaire saw beauty in the rags
Of beggar girls; sickness he deified,
Taking to bed the abscess of the soul.
Man is an esthetic animal.

The human face most seldom is divine
But tends to beast, as nature plans its fall.
God's image, what is left of it, demands
An ignoble etching of authentic line.
The human face unlighted by its sun
Sits in the flesh and sinks in golden mud.
Man is an esthetic animal
And practices the laying-on of hands
Of clay, of sounds, of language and of stone
In imitation of the clay of God.
The human form is seldom beautiful.
Man is an esthetic animal.

The human form is seldom beautiful,
More seldom is the human face divine.
Man is an esthetic animal,
Being the only beast that yearns for style.
Toulouse at the butt-end of his career,
"At last I have forgotten how to draw!"
And then could draw the truly perfect line.
War is an esthetic principle;
The greatest poets have celebrated war.
Man is the victim of esthetic law.
Man is the esthetic animal
Whose human form is seldom beautiful.

The human form is seldom beautiful,
Less beautiful than animal in zoo.
The human mind with beauty is accursed,
Man being esthetic animal.
Man is the only beast that measures busts,
Bottoms and teeth and feet and length of bone.
Man of all living things worships the new,
Man of all creatures thinks he must be first,
Thinks he must intellectualize his lusts.
Man is the only animal alone,
And only man invents his Caliban.
The only esthetic animal is man.

Writer in Exile

Cold and to the north of recognition,
Beyond the kingdom of letters, back-biting banquets,
    Scandals, bequests, laurels and fellowships,
Should I petition the President, kowtow to the Emperor
    From this wasteland of oil-pipes and guns
Where the natives wear skins, speak an unwritten tongue
    And stagger drunk through sleet? Well, here I am,
Writer and poet of international reputation,
    Ironist, sophisticate and wit
Dreaming of oleanders in the sculpture gardens
    And fountains thundering into marble laps,
Equestrian statues of the dear Confederate dead,
    The noble bronzes in the brainwashed blue,
I'm out of it with my highbrow jabs at government,
    Dirty cracks about the chiefs of staff,
Steel industrialists' wives, all that canaille
    Whose favorite word is Honor, the old code word
For guilty. I didn't uproot the sacred olive,
    Poisoned nobody, forged no documents.
Impious perhaps? Neutral during sedition?
    Adulterous? Seducing the minds of matrons?
Undermining the family and the Constitution?
    Loose charges easy to concoct to stick.
I'm stuck with being too familiar with the great,
    Knowing too much, seeing it all and then
Writing it down to amuse myself and tickle the world.
    The world was not amused and I am banished,
Exiled or, as they call it nowadays, *relegated.*
    A truck goes by, bouncing barrels of beer,
Letters are brought; someone writes that my furniture is stolen,
    My house vandalized: signed A Friend. Some friend.
My books are banned from the public libraries, however
    Private copies are circulated and quoted
At cabinet meetings and by Big Chairman himself.
    It snows and snows and makes my fire smoke.
I'm fifty, I'm harmless, I'm good; I'll stand my ground and die;
    My life was moral though my Muse was lax.
The peasants are friendly; I invite them in for a drink,
    Answer their questions about famous temples,
Roads as swift as glass, the Commissar's sexual vices,
    Restaurant prices, rise of the Eastern cults.
Should I write a poem for the Boss in the local dialect,
    Dedicated to the Great Society,

The New Frontier, New Deal, Utopia, whatever,
      Hopefully to get home to climb the marble stairs
Under the Eagle, past the Marines, into the Presence?

The Heiligenstadt Testament

(Beethoven dying)

NOTE: *As the Heiligenstadt Testament, the will in which Beethoven threatened suicide, is one unbroken sentence, so did I conceive of Beethoven's deathbed delirium. The data of the poem are all grounded in fact and may be traced to the* Life *by Alexander Wheelock Thayer, the biography to which all subsequent studies of Beethoven must refer. Thayer was an American. It is tempting to think that Abraham Lincoln may be credited indirectly for the great* Life; *Lincoln appointed Thayer American consul at Trieste, possibly to enable him to pursue the biography.*

Beethoven the man has been mythologized as the great Romantic, revolutionary, etc. The actual Beethoven, on the contrary, was profoundly and conservatively religious, patriotic, cautious, practical and even puritanical.

The first time that he opened me
    with his knife like a pomegranate
I watched my brown blood spurt across the floor
    I was brave I was relieved
        the second time relieved
        the third time I yelled
            call for the priest
    no more get me the priest
            too late too late
    the fire draws the wind
my brother Ludwig died in infancy
        I was next
    and so they named me Ludwig
        he was replaced
I sign my name Louis at times
my mother was a palace servant
    my father a tenor at the court
        and a horrible drunkard
        van is not von
    and passed me off as a *Wunderkind*
        lying about my birth date
            I was no *Wunderkind*
            Beethoven the bungler
I learned to improvise so well on the organ
    at eight because my fingers froze
        my feet froze in the church
since fifteen I have supported
        the entire family
    and am the first to sit with princes
    and summon kings with my baton

                    to the concert hall
        the entire congress of crowned kings
            and would have worn my medal
        beloved medal of the King of France
except somebody said it would rumple my collar
        so did not wear it but left it in my room
            and Waldstein befriended me
                van is not von
        and Haydn wasn't impressed with my playing
                or with me
            the old man's heart breaking
                for the death of Mozart
but I continued my lessons with him
and studied counterpoint in secret
            was Mozart poisoned as they say
by Salieri by competition
                who poisoned my ears
        Waldstein and the Archduke
            played the quartets admirably
            at six o'clock in the morning
I keep time by the motion of their bows
        that way can almost hear my music
            and in some palace or other
        improvise improvise yelled the fools
            and I improvised for the fools
            and when I turned round from the keyboard
                after two hours
some of them were sobbing with ecstasy
            and I stood up and faced them and yelled
                you fools you fools
            I exploded pianos
                big ones little ones
after the gilded horizontal harps
            I needed more octaves
the mahogany thunder was good for my ears
and drowned out the infernal buzzing
                    deaf
                if you are deaf
                and you are Beethoven
                what do you do
            you sing you laugh you dance
            you sing at the top of your voice
that was the way I scared the peasant on the road
        and his oxen bolted and they all bolted

and I sat down and laughed and wept
and my friends detected that I couldn't hear
the shepherd piping close at hand
    and I saw the look in their eyes
      and said nothing
and back at the cottage at Heiligenstadt
    began to write my will
you who think I am malevolent
    stubborn misanthropic
are right because you do not know my secret
I who all my life was the soul of gentleness
    decency and high ambition
      have for six years been suffering
        a permanent malady
the greatest of all imaginable curses
    compelling me to loneliness
      bitterness and despair
for I Beethoven am deaf I am deaf
Beethoven has no ears
how can I say to other men speak louder
    raise your voice
therefore forgive me when I draw away
when I would joyfully mingle with you all
    and hear the shepherd's piping or a cough
    if I could hear a cough
I live in exile when I must approach
    a fellow-man I am seized with horror
suppose that I Beethoven am found out
    and am laughed out of the room
come death quickly come when you will
    and divide my fortune
and I have no wife and my servants are bitches
that follows especially because I am deaf
    how can I hear what they're stealing
yet someone has taken my filthy suit
and left a tailored new one in its place
    enemy or friend
    trust nobody
    because I scribbled
notes on the shutter next the piano
    the landlady has sold the shutters
    to a curious tourist
    and demands that I Beethoven
    pay for new shutters

                    trust nobody
                    especially publishers
        hellhounds that licked and gnawed my brains
        God damn all publishers all but the English
    God bless the English and the Philharmonic
                God bless their national anthem
                the English shamed my publishers
                    into paying me something
                    I saved my money
    40,000 for Karl nobody else
                    thunder lightning and snow
                    all on my deathbed
        that will make for a massive funeral
    for Beethoven 20,000 at the iron gates
        God bless the English they have sent me
        the forty-volume edition of Handel
                Handel the greatest of us all
        they will sing Mozart for my mass
                then Cherubini excellent
                    in excellent taste
                and will close the schools for my funeral
    and 40,000 florins all for Karl
        dear nephew your mother was a whore
    lewdness and irreverence two things beyond me
        and when I took you from her house
                you tried to blow your brains out
                    and almost succeeded
                you don't approve my love
        you steal my manuscripts and sell them
        and run back to your mother the whore
    I did my best to make you hate your mother
        and didn't succeed but you are mine
                    I should have married
        not Bettina Goethe's butterfly
                who fluttered to me from Goethe
    one of those women that collect great men
    bearing the honey of genius mouth to mouth
                her personal mission her errand
    or my immortal beloved I forget her name
        my angel my all my very self
                    my coach broke down in the forest
                    it had only four horses
                    Esterhazy had eight
                    yet I got pleasure from that

overcoming difficulties
remain my true my only treasure
I forget her name
for my Tenth I have it planned
the Goethe Faust
but the old man won't answer my letters
my Ninth I dedicated to the King of Prussia
who in turn gave me a diamond ring
and an innocent bird the yellowhammer
common in Austria as in luscious England
which I shall never see
gave me the theme of my Fifth
I altered the birdsong slightly
and made it the eagle of my pen
the same I did with the singing of peasants
my Battle Symphony my birds
where are my multiplication tables
is it true that any child can understand them
40,000 florins for Karl
let nobody say Beethoven was a fool
too late too late
the fire draws the wind
the wine has not arrived

Moving In

I wish you for your birthday as you are,
Inherently happy,
The little girl always shining out of your face
And the woman standing her ground.

Wish you the seldom oceanic earthquake
Which shatters your gaze
Against some previous interior past
And rights you.

Wish you your honesty normal as a tree
Confounding the caws of intellectuals.
When I zip your dress I kiss you on the neck,
A talisman in honor of your pride.

When I hold your head in my hands
It is as of the roundness of Columbus
Thinking the world, "my hands capable of
Designing the earthly sphere."

Your fingers on the piano keys
Or the typewriter keys or on my face
Write identical transcriptions.
Nothing you do is lost in translation.

I am delighted that you loathe Christmas.
I feel the same way about Communism.
Let us live in the best possible house,
Selfish and true.

May the Verdi *Requiem* continue to knock you out
As it does me; fashionable protest art
Continue to infuriate your heart
And make you spill your drink.

Now ideology has had its day
Nothing is more important than your birthday.
Let us have a solid roof over our head
And bless one another.

Flying First Class

Between the first martini and the wine
A thousand flying-miles
Over the Nevada Flats or Great Salt Lake
Or only a dirty tablecloth of sky,
A navigational turn, the wormy clouds above;
Soon it will be time to dine,
With the clocks wrong among the well-set smiles
Of stewardesses leisurely and ripe.
In first class you can smoke your English pipe.

A gilded drawing of the astrolabe
Brightens the wall of the latrine,
Making me think of that Arabian sage
And Chaucer of a greener age.

The stethoscope pumps music in my ears,
And now they drop a movie screen.

The aluminum wing, the plastic seats, the roar,
The well-dressed heads, perhaps the really rich,
All of us in the friendly arms of kitsch,
Billows of passion—a thunderhead below!
Beef Teriyaki, Caesar Salad Bowl,
Coursing the aureole,
We dream, we worry and we itch.

I see her carving meat across the aisle:
"How do you like your Château?"
Pouring French wine that looks to be
A famous label.

I settle down behind my let-down table
And get three slices of the pink Château,
Wishing I wouldn't think of that Chateaubriand
Whose Atala poisoned herself
For faith, not love,
On the Mississippi where it glints below
Between twin cities of oil and grime;
Better to drift, better to thumb your *Time*.

Fiesta Fruit Plate, coffee, B & B,
Arching from San Francisco to the utmost coasts
In variably empty sky,
Hung there invisibly

314

For banal destinations on the earth
Saturated with all the modern wrongs,
Mal du siècle, the sickness of the age
That God and man and history have wrought.

"Be careful," says the stewardess, "it's hot!"
Handing the small hot towels out on tongs.

Moon Walk

The night before the men walked on the moon
You took the kids to the movies in the dark.
I pondered now if soon
Women would stop their periods and tides
Lie stagnant and the waves desist.

The neighbor behind us is a scientist;
His lights were on and in between them shone
The light leaves of the eucalyptus tree
Whose barely moving tracery
Revealed the spaces of the night that hides.

How quiet are the moon-men at their tasks,
Moving through nothing awesomely.
It is an awesome time when love takes on
The consequences of the untrodden moon.
Awesome it is without you in this room.

The Moss Roses

When wineglasses were flowers (like Tiffany tulips)
And there was stained glass in the dining room
And brown was beautiful,
One would have grown, leaned over, looked at moss roses
(Purslane, porcelaine, *Portulaca grandiflora!*)

Flowers of Art Nouveau! crawling over the slab,
Fluttering like butterflies, three-quarters dead, exotic,
Neo-decadent, succulent, opening soft, shutting at will,
Redon-Gaudí dream-flowers, musical-mystical blooms,
Colors of kleenex, texture of old letter-paper, petals
That flutter like dead moth wings, one at a time,
More than saffron, more than purple, incarnadine,
Waterless white, lustrous cerise, salmon, pastel,
Lavender, orange, pink on the hot dry banks, parking strips,
Gravel beds, patio insets, edgings, in any soil
In the sandy loam, in the terrible heat, self-sown
Low on the ground with stand-still insects sucking,
Insects tiny as smuts in the baby-face jungle,
Drawing the tiny dust-black butterflies, the purslane moths
Amidst the crawly fleshy stems, the edible,
In the Middle Ages used for salads, pickling, curing warts.
And when we pluck them from their bed they undergo
No spectacular suffering, like mandrake or rainbow trout,
But where a while ago they were so thick
We neaten up the plot with crushed red brick.

A Curiosity

Tiny bees come to see what I am,
Lying in the sun at summer's end,
Writing a poem on a reclining chair.
A butterfly approaches and retreats;
Flies bang into my body by mistake,
And tinier things I can't identify;
And now and then a slow gigantic wasp
Rows on its stately voyage to the fence.
The trees are still too little to have birds;
Besides, the neighbors all have special cats
Bred for their oddity or arrogance.
A dragonfly sips at a lemon twig
After a helicopter landing. It
Appears that I am a curiosity
In my own backyard.
The dog of doubtful breed
Sleeps on the carpet of the sod,
And a bee necks with a rose.

Garage Sale

Two ladies sit in the spotless driveway
Casually smoking at the not-for-sale card table,
Over their heads a row of plastic pennants,
Orange, yellow, assorted reds and blues,
Such as flap over used-car lots, a symbol.
Each thing for sale is hand-marked with a label,
And every object shows its homemade bruise.

They sit there all day, sometimes getting up
When a visitor asks a question about a crib
Or a box spring with a broken rib
Or a gas jet to start fireplace fires.

Cars park gently, some with daisy decals,
No Mark IV's, Coupe de Villes or Corvettes;
Mostly wagons with the most copious interiors,
And few if any intellectuals.

All day the shoppers in low-key intensities,
Hoping to find something they are trying to remember
Fits in, or sticks out, approach and mosey,
Buy a coffee mug with a motto, or leave,
And nobody introduces him or herself by name.
That is taboo. And nobody walks fast. That is taboo.
And those who come look more or less the same.

A child buys a baby dress for her Raggedy Anns.
A pair of andirons, a mono hi-fi, a portable
        typewriter, square electric fans,
Things obsolescing but not mature enough to be antiques,
And of course paintings which were once expensive
Go or can go for a song.

This situation, this neighborly implosion,
As flat as the wallpaper of Matisse
Strikes one as a cultural masterpiece.
In this scene nothing serious can go wrong.

California Petrarchan

I hear the sunset ambulances surround
Suburbia at the turquoise edge of day,
Loping along the not-too-far freeway
Where olive trees and red bloodshed abound.
The oleanders with a shore-like sound
Perform their dance beside my own driveway
As if they also had a word to say
In all their whiteness beautifully gowned.

This Italy with insanity all its own
Lacks only history to make it true
And bitterness that ripens hour by hour.
This baby Italy, more straw than stone,
Stumbling, choking, fighting toward the New,
Bursts into flame with its own fire power.

Death of the Fig

In troublous night the wind took out the fig
With a flying tackle, with a rapist's leap,
And laid it on the ground, wrecked at the base,
Thick and silvery, unconscious and prostrate
With all its fat green foliage, fat white figs.
By morning the fat fruit begins to drop
Like surrealist raindrops, by ten o'clock
The leaves begin to scrunch and die
A very sudden and immediate death.
I walk around it like an auto wreck
Muttering goddammit and get the pruning saw
Curved like a scimitar to waste the tree.
Flies are already gathering on the fruit,
Mashed honey-bellies, honey-leaking glands.
I saw as if in a tremendous hurry,
Becoming frenzied, using a larger saw,
Rose-clippers for twigs, wearing me out.
Now there's a yellow bee, now two or three
Burrowing into the pulp, signaling me
To hold it or give them a chance, or else
(Somebody is going to have some white-fig honey).
And finally I stack the sticky wood
Leaving three feet of trunk and four branch stumps,
A mutilate, a monster upsidedown,
Four-legged cripple without head
To paint with luminous paint for Halloween
Beside the front-door pumpkin, trick or treat.

The Piano Tuner's Wife

That note comes clear, like water running clear,
Then the next higher note, and up and up
And more and more, with now and then a chord,
The highest notes like tapping a tile with a hammer,
Now and again an arpeggio, a theme,
As if the keyboard spoke to the one key,
Saying, No interval is exactly true,
And the note whines slightly and then truly sings.

She sits on the sofa reading a book she has brought,
A ray of sunlight on her white hair.
She is here because he is blind. She drives.
It is almost a platitude to say
That she leads him from piano to piano.

And this continues for about an hour,
Building bridges from both sides of the void,
Coasting the chasms of the harmonies.

And in conclusion,
When there is no more audible dissent,
He plays his comprehensive keyboard song,
The loud proud paradigm,
The one work of art without content.

Sestina: of the Militant Vocabulary

The first word you must know is *relevant,*
The qualifier of *experience.*
Relevant experience of the *revolution,*
For instance, trains you to confront the *pigs,*
The first defense line of the *power structure,*
Which guards insidiously the *Establishment.*

What we are after is the Establishment,
Which acts as if we are not relevant
And forces us to wreck the power structure.
This confrontation is an experience
Not only for the people but for the pigs
Whom we'll win over in the revolution.

When we make love we make the revolution,
As war is made by the Establishment,
For in our confrontation with the pigs
We prove to them that they're irrelevant
And immaterial to the experience,
Which in itself can wreck the power structure.

The military-industrial power structure,
A major target of the revolution,
Must also be a sexual experience.
To expose the symbols of the Establishment
Expose yourself—it's highly relevant
And absolutely petrifies the pigs.

In our utopia there will be no pigs
And no remains of any power structure
Except what we decide is relevant;
And what is relevant but revolution?
We spell the death of the Establishment,
Which will probably welcome the experience.

Meanwhile, experience the experience;
Demand, demand, and overwhelm the pigs
Till we in fact are the Establishment
And constitute a groovy power structure.
Remember the slogan of the revolution:
Now is forever; Now is relevant.

While pigs perpetuate the power structure,
Baby, be relevant to the revolution
Till we experience the Establishment.

Death of the Yamoto

(April, 1945)

Out of the Inland Sea
Into the Eagle's claws
We sail to suicide.

Yamoto, biggest battleship ever built,
Most beautiful to commit
The biggest suicide of all.

Only the Floating Chrysanthemums remain,
Petals drifting into American flak,
To die for the Emperor.

Their ships rose up from Pearl like ghosts,
Their wings blacken the sun;
We proceed to our dying.

Yamoto they say is unsinkable,
Our sister-ship *Mushashi* was unsinkable
But heeled over and sank.

An American admiral Morrison writes of us,
Singularly beautiful ship,
A graceful sheer to her flush deck

Unbroken from stem to stern
With streamlined mast and stack,
Seventy thousand tons of steel.
Yamoto means Japan.

War is like kendo with bamboo spears,
War is like haiku for surprise;
The sudden stroke at Pearl, at Singapore,
Philippines, Malaysia,
All the way to our own great south,
But after that, no more surprises.

Yet even now the Divine Wind
That sank the ships of Genghis Khan
Might bring us peace with honor
And quench the Flowers of Edo
That burn our people in their beds.

When we had sunk *Repulse* and *Prince of Wales*
We did not strafe the watery survivors,
Instead dropped flowers on the waves;
One could be gracious in the early days.

We speak no more of the Decisive Battle;
If ever there was a Decisive Battle
It is on the deck of an American ship.
Hellcats and Avengers coming on,
Bombers at all points of the clock,
We are fueled for one way only.

Pagoda masts as visible as Fuji,
Two hundred and eight star-planes coming on,
Mainmast hit, return fire defective,
No live practice any more.

Five torpedo hits, starboard engine,
Boiler room flooded,
Several hundred seamen trapped,
Caught between cold water,
Boiling water, steam,
List not corrected, wireless room flooded,
Flag and light signals all that's left,
Decks a shambles, cracked and twisted steel,
Coral color from internal heat,
Big guns inoperable.

Blast in dispensary kills all present,
Doctors and corpsmen as well,
Communications ended from the bridge,

Distress flag hoisted, steering room flooded,
Rudder jammed hard left,
List thirty-five degrees.

Final conference of available staff,
Salutes, bows, prolonged silence,
Shaking of hands, singing and tears.

Deck nearly vertical,
Battle flag touching the waves,
Skidding shells kindling explosions,
Yamoto sliding completely under.

326

Blast, rumble and shock of compartments,
Bursting from air pressure, magazines exploding,
Complement of two thousand sixty-seven men.

No word for *surrender* in our Code,
No word for *retreat,*
Only *Yamoto.*

The Rape of Philomel

1

Procne said, it happened at my wedding
On the wedding night in the bedroom
Foul influences presided
Juno was not there
Hymen was not there
Nor the three Graces in the bride-room
But the Furies came
With fire stolen from a funeral
And a screech owl screamed up in the rafters
Over the bride-bed
While Tereus my husband took my body
And the owl splattered us naked
And that same night I conceived my son
Itys, Itys
And for five years was a peaceful wife
A dutiful queen but begged my husband
Tereus I miss my sister
Send me to Philomel or her to me
It makes no difference which
And with my flesh persuaded him
To send me to Athens or her to Thrace
Till finally Tereus sailed to Athens
Over the curling sea in his king's ship
To bring my sister Philomel
To me to see each other and compare.

2

Philomel said, when the king came
I mean Tereus my sister's king
He grasped my father's hand, hands of two kings,
And stated his errand that I sail back
To visit Procne in her own palace
But when my father called me to enter
Tereus' eyes gloated, I felt undressed
He scanned my clothes and underneath my clothes
He sweated, he sighed, he stared
His eyes glued to my flesh
Men of his country are notorious for that
He talked too fast, his words foamed
His lips boiled, his eyes wetted
Yet he seemed kind and reverent and soft
I begged my father let me go
O let me go with Tereus to my dear

Which my good father nodded at with frowns
And sob-shaken saw us aboard.

3

Tereus said, it was a common errand
Though generous for me
To fetch my sister-in-law to see my queen
A visit of alliance, courtesy
And so I sailed the curling sea to Athens
Pleaded with Pandion the king
To hand his daughter Philomel
Into my trust to bear her to her flesh
Her flesh-and-blood her sister, my queen
And he acceded but when she entered
My blood took fire my insides roiled
Like animals let loose I lost my footing
My brain was like a barn-fire
I thought I'd bribe her nurses have her now
Offer her the richest whore's gold
Or rape her in her room and if I die
What difference does it make, somehow I spoke
The right words and got her to the ship
Shook hands and embraced the king
Who wept to see her go as well he might.

4

Philomel said, why on his ship
Did Tereus' eyes dog me like a thief
Silkily following my every move
Or now like an eagle gazing down
As if I were a rabbit to be snatched
By ripping claws borne to his crag.

5

Tereus said, the swift ship finally
Has struck the shore of Thrace, I have her bound
And wrenched to the hut in the black wood
Hurl her down and rip her dress to threads
And mount her like a whore
The more she cries for Procne or her father
Riper more frantic grows my lust
And now she prays and quakes like a lamb
Torn by a wolf or bloodied like a dove

Maimed by a hawk, she tears her hair
Claws at her arms and shrieks her hate
And swears revenge for Procne for herself
Her father for broken vows, for fate
She shall be sworn to all the gods
Till rocks shed tears and stones repeat
The rape of Philomel, till in my rage
I yanked her tongue forth with a pincers
And with my dagger cut it off
Where it lay throbbing at her feet as if
To creep back to its mistress, foul thing
Twitching like a serpent's tail, and watching
I mounted her again and gorged my pleasure.

6

Procne said, my sister fell asleep
On board Tereus' ship and a tall wave
As if for love of her in all her beauty
Curled over her and took her in its arms
And bore her down to bottomless sleep,
Tereus told me this with howling moans
And is disconsolate and hunts each day
In the dark wood to control his sorrow,
As for me I dress in black
And go to see the sepulchre I built
To pray and do the rites of my dear dead
Sister Philomel.

7

Philomel thought, I will pick out old threads
And weave my story in the frame
For Procne's eyes to read
The old servant will take it to the queen
A present from an unknown hand.

8

Procne said, when I unwound the gift
And read the poison of the truth
I locked myself in a far room and wept
Plotted our revenge and held my tongue

But on the feast of Bacchus when the night
Shakes with clash of brass and women's shrieks
Rip through the sky and animals are caught

And torn apart and eaten and perhaps
Even a child is caught and torn and eaten
I dressed as Frenzy with the Thracian women
Vines in my hair the deerskin on my back
Spear at my shoulder, mad with grief
I raced the forest to her cottage
And screaming Bacchus Bacchus smashed the door
And dressed my Philomel as a Bacchante
All draped with ivy and ripe vines
And brought her in terror to the palace
Hid her in a farthest room to weep
In one another's arms and plot the end
How? to burn the palace down
And Tereus in its ruins, use the sword?
Torture his body, stick out his eyes,
Hack him to pieces, cut off his genitals
That have raped all of us and Thrace?
At which my sole son Itys wandered by
Itys the image of Tereus, Itys
His heir, I hugged him close and kissed him
Merely my child, a prince, a monster's child
Then Philomel took down a sword for me
I stabbed him through the breast
And my crazed sister seized the sword
And stabbed him through the throat, the room ran blood,
We cut and pared the boy and threw the gobbets
Into the cooking pots and boiled the meat
Itys' hacked head staring from the table.

9

Tereus said, it is my privilege
This black night of the orgies to be served
Alone upon my throne by my good queen
Who this night is my sole servant
And eat whatever food she sets at table
And after eating to admit my son
Who someday will repeat the privilege,
Bring Itys here.

10

Procne said, you have your Itys here
Inside you, flesh of your flesh
It is your son you ate for privilege
Monster tyrant rapist
Now you have feasted on your flesh and blood,
At which with foaming lips and splashed with gore
Philomel leapt before the king and flung
The dripping boy's head at his father's head
Whose face a map of horror staggered up
And tried to vomit but pulled out his sword.

Fly Philomel I screamed and both of us
Flew down the hallways, suddenly on wings
For Philomel was a nightingale
And I a swallow slicing through the air
And King Tereus with a helmet's crest
And bill shaped like a spear
Leapt in the air to follow us.

The feathers of these birds are stained with murder.

Index of Titles

Index of First Lines

About the Author

KARL SHAPIRO was born in Baltimore, Maryland, and attended the University of Virginia and Johns Hopkins University. In 1946 he was appointed Consultant in Poetry at the Library of Congress, and then, in 1947, he joined the faculty of Johns Hopkins University, where he taught writing courses. From 1950 to 1956 he was editor of *Poetry: A Magazine of Verse.* He was Professor of English and editor of *The Prairie Schooner* at the University of Nebraska from 1956 to 1966, and professor of English at the Chicago Circle Campus of the University of Illinois from 1966 to 1968. He is now professor of English at the University of California at Davis. He is a member of the National Institute of Arts and Letters. His second volume of verse, *V-Letter and Other Poems,* was awarded the Pulitzer Prize in 1945. He was awarded the Bollingen Prize in Poetry in 1969.

7